Upon
a
River Bank

By the same author

Salmon and Trout
Scotland's King of Fish
Introduction to Freshwater Ecology
The Fishing Here is Great!
Ecology and Management of Atlantic Salmon
The Salmon Rivers of Scotland (with Neil Graesser)
Freshwater Ecology (with Michael Jeffries)
Strategies for the Rehabilitation of Salmon Rivers (editor)
Salmon in the Sea and New Enhancement Strategies (editor)
The Ocean Life of Atlantic Salmon (editor)
Salmon at the Edge (editor)

Available from:
Coch-y-Bonddu Books, Machynlleth, Wales, SY20 8DJ, UK.
Tel: 01654 702837   Fax: 01654 702857
paul@anglebooks.com   www.anglebooks.com

Published by Derek Mills.

Photographs by the author

ISBN 1-904784-01-1

Printed by Meigle Colour Printers Ltd., Tweedbank Industrial Estate,Galashiels,
TD1 3RS, Scotland, UK.

To Jenny for all her encouragement and advice and
to Richard for his constant companionship on the river bank.

Upon a River Bank

By Derek Mills

Upon a river bank serene
A fisher sat where all was green
  And looked it.

He saw when light was growing dim
A fish or else the fish saw him,
  And hooked it.

He took with high erected comb,
The fish or else the story home,
  And cooked it.

Recording angels by his bed,
Heard all that he had done or said,
  And booked it.

(Anon)

List of Contents

Preface

A short time ago our daughter, Jenny, was looking through some of the articles I had written for the *Flyfishers' Journal* over the years and suggested that these should be put together as a book. It was apparent that there were too few to make a volume of any substance. I therefore set about writing a few more to make it more substantial and while doing this more angling experiences came to mind and so more chapters materialised. I also began to realise that I had been very privileged to fish in so many places since my early beginnings in the 1930s. I owe this enjoyment to a splendid group of friends and to good health. Our son, Richard, has been a tremendous companion on very many outings at home and abroad. There were times when I would have stayed by the fire with a book had it not been for his insistence that we should go fishing.

Looking through my logbooks it soon became noticeable that over the years the angling scene has gradually changed. The angler may notice these changes which are then simply ignored or taken for granted. His demand for large fish and exotic places to ply his art is to be expected, but it is rather sad that one can't be satisfied with more modest aspirations. His equipment, too, has become very sophisticated and very attainable through mail order. Sadly the traditional fishing tackle shop is almost a thing of the past and where it does exist most of its stock consists of clothing rather than fishing gear. Perhaps there is nothing surprising in this and these changes must be accepted as part of our social history. There are very many more people on our Globe since I first started fishing and the wilderness experience is less easy to find. People pop up in the most unlikely places at the most unusual times. Man's impact on the environment and its plants and animals, too, has been very damaging. There are now signs that he realises this and is trying hard to make amends. It will take time. Some animals may never reach their previous numbers. It has been wonderful to grow up in those "good old" days and to have fished peacefully in unspoiled countryside. Let's hope our children and our children's children too will have the opportunity to fish peacefully and unmolested in an improved environment.

I should like to thank the Flyfishers' Club for allowing me to use some of my articles that have appeared in their *Journal* from time to time. I am particularly grateful to their editor, Kenneth Robson for his encouragement. The names of all those who have provided me with fishing or put me in the way of it are too numerous to list. I thank them all. I should particularly like to thank my students for keeping me young at heart and preserving my sense of humour. Acknowledgements would not be complete without thanking my wife, Florence, for her companionship and forbearance on many fishing outings throughout our married life.

Derek Mills.

May, 2004.

Chapter 1 – **Spring Salmon**

Although it was only 26th January there was a feeling of spring in the air. There had been some severe weather until the last few days but now the air was warm and the great tits were actually singing. It was the opening day of the rod season on the Conon and Jimmy Younger senior and I reached the river to see ice floes of varying sizes, some almost as big as billiard tables, coming down the river. We were on the Slaggan, a good pool on the lower river and only a short distance from tidal influence. We were not despondent as the Conon in those days usually produced a fish or two on the opening day.

The simpler the rig in spinning the better; a ball-bearing swivel about 18 inches above the lure, which was usually a wooden devon minnow. The devon we used was one of Jimmy's making and was flatter and more sprat-like than the conventional round ones. These flat ones tended to flutter rather than spin monotonously. Their colour was usually brown and gold although black and gold was quite a good alternative. The gold of the belly was produced by gluing on gold 'silver' paper and then adding a clear varnish – most attractive. It was best to put on a spiral or foldover lead above the swivel. This meant that the weight bounced across the river bed and the wooden devon fished a foot or so above, so when you felt the lead bouncing across the bottom you knew the lure was fishing effectively. The hole through the devon was large enough to be able to slide a tubular lead on to the wire mount, so that if the river was high the bait got down quickly. It was best to cast slightly upstream to allow the bait to be fishing by the time it was opposite you. A word of warning, this method is not suitable for all rivers and the chances of getting hung-up on the bottom are higher on some rivers than others. We did get hung-up from time to time but Jimmy had made a very efficient "otter" out of wood and wedge-shaped. One of the narrow sides of the wedge was weighted with lead along its length and a slot was cut diagonally into the wedge ending in a small hole. So when you were fast on the bottom you slid your line into the slot and prevented it from coming out by putting a peg, secured to the side of the wedge by a short piece of cord, into a hole drilled across the slot. The "otter" floated out, pointed end first, and worked its way across to beyond the point at which the bait was snagged and created a pull from the opposite side. The result almost every time was the freeing of the bait. I set up this wooden devon 'rig' on Tweed but when the boatman saw it he immediately dismantled it and put on the ubiquitous Toby of so many grams!

Casting to avoid the ice floes, it was not long before I had a distinct heavy pull. My first thought was – kelt. However, a more dogged fight dismissed this thought and a clean fish came into the side. It was a small fish of only 5lb. Duncan McIntosh, superintendent of the Conon Salmon District Fishery Board, had a heavier fish at almost the same time from the Little Junction higher up the river. That was that, although Jimmy and I had six sea trout up to 3lb and numerous kelts up to early afternoon and then everything went quiet.

Frost, snow and ice are no deterrent to success and I've seen lower Tweed so covered in snow grue that the lure just landed on top of it and it was impossible to fish. When it moved during the day when a wind got up, one could get the lure into the water and then often caught fish. Even a bitterly cold wind is no deterrent to catching fish although it may make them very sluggish. On one occasion on the Conon a fish I hooked came close to the surface, turned on its side and just fluttered and allowed itself to be netted without a struggle, it weighed 11½lb. Fishing in a snowstorm can be quite productive. It may have something to do with a rise in air temperature when it starts to snow. Orme Armstrong, who was a keen local angler, was fishing with a group of anglers on the lower Conon on a day of heavy snow showers. They were all sheltering in the fishing hut during a particularly heavy shower when Orme asked if they minded if he went off to fish the Top Box, a good little holding pool. They all thought he was crazy, that is until he came back shortly afterwards with a clean fish. However, nothing would stir his friends so he said he would give it another try rather than to sit about doing nothing. Again, another fish was brought back to the hut. When he said he would go again if no one was going to move they laughed and said a fluke couldn't happen three times – but it did!

In the first two or three months of the season on the Conon one always caught a large number of kelts. It at least gave one some sport and one never knew, on first hooking the fish, whether it was going to be a kelt or a clean fish. There were a number of what we called 'kelt holes' on the river which were notorious for the number of kelts they produced. However, they were always fished, as they had been known, on numerous occasions, to yield a springer. There were times when all one caught in the morning were kelts and then, for some inexplicable reason, perhaps change in air temperature, clean fish were taken after lunch in the same pools that one had fished in the morning and from which one had only taken kelts. Kelts were always treated pretty peremptorily. However, one could have surprises. Once fishing the little River Kanaird on the west coast in April I hooked what I believed to be a kelt and, as spring fish were uncommon on west coast rivers, I didn't give the fish 'its head' but brought it in unceremoniously. Imagine my surprise when I stared in astonishment at a beautiful clean 9lb springer lying gasping at my feet!

Some of the nicest spring fishing one can have is on the rivers in Sutherland. They are all of a size at which one can get to know them intimately. This is quite different to the larger rivers such as the Tweed and Tay. Fishing lower Tweed in the spring usually involves fishing from a boat. In cold weather this is uncomfortable and one is at the mercy of the boatman who is not in the boat but is roping you from the shore. The first time I experienced this and, not knowing the procedure, I began fishing and then opened up a conversation. Getting no replies to my various remarks, I turned round and found no one in the boat! A length of rope extended from the boat to the "boatman" on the bank who had the other end of the rope round his waist. The pool I was fishing was very exposed and a cold east wind was blowing through me. There was nothing one could do but keep casting out my Toby spoon and hoping that my "guardian" would decide that he had had enough and lower me to the end of the pool as quickly as possible – fish or no fish. However, things are better on a warm day in May when one has the swallows and sand martins to keep one company. I have rarely fished the Tay in spring and on the one occasion that I did it involved harling. This is a method where you sit in the boat which is rowed or, more likely, propelled through the water with the aid of an outboard motor. One or two rods with lures trailing from them are leaning against the stern. The 'angler' sits and waits for a fish to hook itself and in the meantime freezes.

The lower Cassley, owned by my old pal Neil Graesser, was a delight to fish in the spring. Neil had spent a great deal of time improving the pools with the installation of gabions and a casting stance at the Upper Platform. April was

3

usually a productive month and visits then yielded fish from the Round Pool, the Run, Upper and Lower Platform, the Pot and the Dipper. The fish were all fresh in from the Kyle. The flies in general use were the Collie Dog and Tadpole in various sizes, all tied with hair from the local collie dogs. Neil used silver trebles that tended to be softer than bronze ones and had a habit of bending after playing an energetic fish or if one's fly hit a boulder while casting. So it was important to check hooks regularly. The river was of a width where my 13ft Sharpes spliced impregnated cane rod was all that was needed, although an extra foot would have been useful to present the fly more effectively on the Round Pool. Some folk were using 16ft carbon fibre rods and, although the extra length was not necessary, the lightness of carbon fibre made for a less tiring day. However, I found that a cane rod tires a fish more quickly but, at the same time, a cane rod tires the angler more quickly unless he has young strong arms and shoulders!

The routine at lunchtime in the bar of Neil's local hostelry was a friendly interrogation of one's activities with fish that morning. Neil had a range of questions. What fly, what time was it caught, which pool and whereabouts in the pool, how did it take? And so on. This was a pleasant way of spending a sandwich lunch and renewing the morning's fishing experiences. One was always improving one's fishing when with Neil. A successful method he had of fishing a pool, after fishing it down, was to back it up. Backing it up often rewarded a fishless run down the pool. I have copies of all three books he wrote on salmon fishing and find them invaluable. They are: *Fly Fishing for Salmon, Advanced Salmon Fishing* and *The Finer Points of Fly Fishing for Salmon*.

My first introduction to the Brora was with Neil Graesser when we fished the lower beat below Loch Brora with some success. However, it was the experience of a lifetime to fish this river above the loch and its major tributary, the Black Water. I was invited by Richard Tyser on three occasions to stay with him at Gordonbush Lodge in April and fish this section of the river. It was a privilege and a pleasure. My first visit was the most memorable. The river had been low for some time and on the first morning I was sent off with a flask of coffee to fish the Black Water where there would be a chance of a fish at the Balnacoil Falls Pool. Richard would join me about mid-day with the lunch. As there was no ghillie I was 'my own man'. This meant that I could fish at my own pace. Much as I like ghillies I find one has to keep fishing and is unable to relax. On my own, I frequently rest, have a cup of coffee and, if the car is handy, sit and read for a while. This may sound like sacrilege to some 'keen' anglers but I can assure them that it's most relaxing and doesn't necessarily mean fewer fish on the bank. The morning went in quite quickly and Richard soon appeared with the lunch. We were standing by the Pheadair Pool by Balnacoil Lodge and Richard remarked that if there were a rise in water I would be hauling the fish out from this pool. I thought he was exaggerating but little knew how right he was! A leisurely lunch and then I was directed to MacDonald's Pool which Richard's sister and the ghillie were leaving on my arrival. Yes, there was a fish there but it wouldn't take. One of Neil Graesser's 1½in. Tadpoles seemed a good bet and half way down the pool there was a slight twitching of the line which was then gently pulled out. On duly tightening a fish bored sullenly across the pool but, with little current, it was soon drawn into the side and netted - 7½lb. As there was no more activity a move was made down the river to the Snag where, because of the gradient, there was quite a bit of current. A change of fly seemed appropriate and 1 inch Adam's Fancy took the place of the Tadpole. It was a nice pool to fish and it was not long before the line went off smartish and a good struggle ensued. Soon there was another 7½lb clean fish on the bank. Richard arrived and thought that other pools would be better fished when there was more water, which he predicted would arrive next day. So stumps were drawn and we retired to the house for tea

There had been some rain during the night and this, together with the melting snow from Ben Armine, had raised the river level slightly. What was needed now was some hot sun to continue the snow melting process, and this would come. The Pheadair was coming to a nice fishable height and most of the day was spent fishing this over a number of times in a fairly leisurely way. Over the course of the day I took four clean fish of 6½, 7½, 8½ and 9lb on a 1½ inch Tadpole, a 1 inch Adam's Fancy and a 1 inch Garry Dog. As the river was still rising I packed up early with the feeling that things were 'hotting up' for the next day.

The river had risen appreciably overnight and the Pheadair was at a good fishable level in the morning. The sun was shining and I could imagine the snow beginning to recede on Ben Armine. A bigger fly was called for and a 2 inch Tadpole was tied on. The river was too high for wading and really a 16ft rod was called for, but as I only had my 13ft Sharpe's spliced cane rod a lot of 'beef' had to go into casting. However, there was all the time in the world and, as I was the only rod, one could take it leisurely up to a point, as sport was fast and furious. The fish took well all morning and early afternoon and then activity ceased but not before I had seven on the bank – 6, 6½, 6½, 7, 8½, 8½ and 9.

Next day three of us were on the river, Richard, Mr. Aldenham and myself. The river was still running at a good height. The total catch for the day was 20. Most fell to Richard's rod as, like his mother, Jessie Tyser, he is an excellent angler. Four fish came my way, all taken on a Willie Gunn Waddington.

The next, and final, day was a bonanza. The morning was fine and sunny and the river was now running at a nice height. Richard hoped to join me later. Starting off on the right bank of the Pheadair it was all systems go right from

Spring salmon from the River Brora, Sutherland

the start and it was more like trout fishing. In not more than an hour I had caught six salmon. Now I knew what Richard meant when he said that if this pool was at the right height one would be hauling them out! Shortly after moving over to the left bank, Richard arrived and, after seeing my catch went over to the Flat Pool below the confluence of the Black Water and Brora. He suggested that, as the river was now less turbulent below the Falls, I try the Falls and also the Struan, which is just upstream of the Pheadair. I was fishing a 2 inch Willie Gunn and this weight of fly was definitely needed in the Falls Pool. Practically as soon as the fly sunk there would be a strong pull and the fish seemed to be queuing up to take the fly. After landing two, one weighing 11lb, I moved down to the Struan. This is a lovely short pool and just shouts "fish". A fish took with a bang and shot off down to the Pheadair and it must have been the best part of 100 metres before I got on terms with it. It weighed 11½lb. One became rather blasé about landing fish and where possible one just beached them. The next one I took from the Pheadair I "beached" on a rock some distance out from the bank and then waded out and tailed it. Richard was getting down to work on the Flat Pool and, at his invitation, I joined him and here caught my last fish of the day, number 12. Richard's sister was fishing another part of the river and doing equally well. Our score for the day was 23. My twelve weighed, 6, 6, 7, 7, 7, 7, 8½, 8½, 8½, 9½, 11 and 11½lb - 97½lb - a record day. This brought my total for the five days fishing to 23 fish weighing 227½lb.

The following day the rods caught no fish. The fish, which had been travelling, had probably all passed upstream over the Falls. As I drove past Loch Brora on my way south a large skein of greylag geese were flying north, it would soon be summer.

Chapter 2 – **Summer on the Little Gruinard**

Garve in Easter Ross lies at the gateway to the West Coast. Just after this little village, and driving west, take the right hand fork in the road and you are on the road to Ullapool. The road used to be single track with passing places or laybys that all tourists seemed to ignore unless they stopped in them for a picnic. It was an attractive route and one we all enjoyed on our way to the Little Gruinard and the home of James Lawrie. On the right, just before Garbat, rose Ben Wyvis with its resident golden eagles, then Glascarnoch Reservoir and its dam constructed by the North of Scotland Hydro-electric Board and beyond lay little Loch Droma. Just before Corrieshalloch Gorge and the Falls of Measach one turned sharp left and drove along by Little Loch Broom with An Teallach massif on your left. After a steep drive up and away from Little Loch Broom one turned the corner going left and came down to the lovely Gruinard Bay. After crossing the Big Gruinard River the road comes right down to the sands and at the base of the hill leading up to Aultbea and on to Poolewe and Gairloch one turned in at a gate on the right and came down to the Lawrie's house.

There is a path from the attractive white house that leads down to the river. Keep straight on and it takes you down to the sea. The river flows gently into the bay after a torrential fall from the bridge down to the Garden Pool. Here it divides at an island and joins up again just above Harry's Run before turning sharp left into the Nut Pool and then down into the Sea Pool which is flooded out by the sea at high tide. On a summer's evening the Bay is very peaceful with the river flowing out to sea and a small sandy beach along the left bank. One can frequently hear the black-throated divers calling as they come down from the hill lochs where they are nesting. When the weather is very still dolphins can occasionally be heard blowing. But when it is as still as that the midges are so bad that one is driven indoors.

The morning following the day of our arrival was lovely and warm with just enough cloud to prevent a glare coming off the water and a gentle breeze to put a ripple on the pools of the Flats which was the destination later in the day. My equipment was a 13ft Sharpes spliced impregnated cane rod, a reel with a floating line, a box of flies and a spool of 8lb nylon. A game bag, containing a flask of tea and sandwiches and a couple of straw basses to carry any fish, should luck come my way, was slung over my shoulder. Although there was a long walk ahead, waders were unfortunately necessary as there were some pools that would need wading. After crossing the road and passing through the gate there was a half-mile walk along a narrow rough track before reaching the first fishable pool at the present water height, the Knoll.

The Knoll looked most attractive. The river was at the right height so that all boulders were covered and there was a slightly peaty tinge in the water. My favourite fly, a Blue Charm, was tied on and, because of the river level, a largish size was felt necessary. There is always a sense of excitement on making the first cast at the beginning of a week that seemed very promising. The pool was fished down more than half way before there was a welcome pull on the line and fun had started. The strong current was all in favour of the fish. Gradually the gleam of a silvery flank as the fish turned on its side showed that it was tiring. Two or three more desperate struggles with the line being taken out and the tired fish beginning to float down to the tail of the pool heralded the end of the fight and, wading in, the fish was tailed and laid on the bank. It was a beautiful fresh-run fish as bright as polished silver with a deep blue back, a few black spots along its flanks and the odd sea louse, a hallmark of recent sojourn in the sea. This was no grilse but a large summer salmon of 10½lb. After fishing out the remainder of the pool, and as a long walk was still ahead of me, the salmon was gently laid on a nearby heather-clad rock and, covered with sprigs of bog myrtle, and left for collection on my return.

The Major's Pool, about a quarter of a mile further upstream, was in nice order. Fish tend to lie towards the right bank where there is a small rocky ledge. This pool was usually rewarding and today was no exception and a nice 7lb. salmon was soon on the bank and hidden by the path for me to uplift later. There was no point lugging it up to the Flats, which were now, a long steep uphill hoof with the river running down a steep gorge. On reaching level ground at the top of the hill one has to leave the track, which is no more than a sheep track, and head diagonally across boggy ground to the lower Flats. These start off at the head of a bend in the river and continue in a long pool widening towards the end where it is broken up by boulders on the right bank. It is all good water with plenty of lies for fish that are able to rest after negotiating the strong flow in the gorge. As the current was much less here a change was made to a size 10 Yellow Dog. This is a Garry Dog without the red hair in the wing. An experienced angler, Orme Armstrong, from Strathconon, tied this particular fly. The yellow wing is made of floss silk rather than deer hair. It is very visible in peaty water. Starting at the top of the Flats, where today there was a nice gentle flow along the right bank lined with rushes, it was not long before there was a pull on the line and a good fight ensued before another fresh 7lb. salmon was tailed. There was no further excitement on the Lower Flats, although some fish were showing, so a gentle climb was made to the Middle Flats where by now it was time for a break and some refreshment.

The Middle Flats consist of a fairly short wide still pool, with the river coming in at the top through a number of small islands. It has a peaty bed and is a very good resting-place for fish that have negotiated a steep swim through rough water from the Lower Flats. The pool fishes best when there is a gentle downstream breeze, which there was today. The best way to fish the pool is, starting at the top, to cast diagonally across and slowly retrieve the line. Today the result was magical and three grilse were taken in quick succession. The banks are a little unstable but there was a convenient little side drain leading into the pool and fish were drawn into this and tailed. The fish had been in the river for a few days and were much of a size, 6, 6 and 5lb. All were taken on the Yellow Dog. The morning had gone in very pleasantly and it was now definitely time for lunch and a rest. A nice heather-covered knoll by the tail of the pool was a good resting-place and one had a lovely view up the strath towards the hills in which nestled, out of sight, the remote Fionn Loch. It was so peaceful that it was as though one was the only person in the world. There was no sound of traffic or low-flying aircraft and only the slight lapping of the water against the riverbanks and the occasional splash of a fish broke the silence. The hills in the distance were like sleeping dinosaurs with the clouds caressing their backs. I woke with a start. My rod and the fish were still lying near me and the sun was still shining. A doze of a few minutes can be very refreshing. The flask of tea was finished and it was time for one more fish. A few half-hearted plucks at the fly and then a fierce tug and a small silvery grilse jumped clear of the water. A good struggle ensued before it was finally tailed. It was a small fish of 4¼lb. It was to be a long walk back and there were five fish to carry and two more to pick up on the way. Thank goodness for a game bag and two basses! It had been a good day all round,

Florence and the children had had a great day on the beach and yours truly had a "high erected comb"!

I fished the Middle Flats on the following two days as the river was remaining at a good fishable height and the weather was settled with sunshine and a gentle breeze. This suited the family as the tide was right for a good spell on the beach. The Middle Flats yielded four fish on each day, all to the Yellow Dog. Three of these were salmon of 9¾lb., 9¼lb. and 7lb. The largest of the three was heavily spotted. At that time there were no salmon farms on the West Coast, so it was not an escaped farmed salmon but a previous spawner which are frequently more heavily spotted. This was confirmed by the presence of white maggots on its gills. The grilse weights ranged from 5¾ to 3½lb.

The weather continued fine so we all went down to the beach, and while the family were playing, a cast in the Sea Pool seemed to be in order. A few fish were coming in and soon one took my Blue Charm and about-turned and tore out to sea. It was possible to follow it so far then the water became too deep. The fish could be seen wallowing in the tangle as seaweed is called on the West Coast. There was no way it could be dislodged and we soon parted company. This often happens on Sea Pools! Although this river is not frequented by many sea trout the odd heavy fish is recorded. However, the Sea Pool was a good place for finnock and Richard caught quite a few which encouraged him for greater things. They were also a good addition to the breakfast table.

To vary the routine and as the weather was exceptionally good and the sea very calm; James Lawrie prepared his rowing boat complete with outboard motor for a spell of sea fishing. After gathering mussels from the neighbouring rocks we took to the briny and motored out to some good offhsore marks which haddock were known to frequent. Handlines and terminal tackle on an old cane spinning rod were baited with mussels and lowered over the side and held in anticipation. It was not long before expected tugs started and lines were hauled up eagerly. One never knows in sea fishing just what is at the end of one's line until it is hauled aboard. In our case the fish were chiefly haddock and Richard had an exceptionally large specimen in excess of 3½lb. Porpoises were about and their blowing at the surface was quite distinct. They were quite near Gruinard Isle where experimental germ warfare was carried out during the Second World War. Sadly the island is still contaminated with anthrax spores and is officially out of bounds.

At exceptionally low tide we would go over to the main beach with small garden rakes to scrape the sand to expose the cockles. These were then gathered and taken back and placed in a basin of cold water in which they opened the valves of their shells and cleansed themselves before dying. They were gently boiled and eaten with brown bread and butter. Another shellfish that was literally chased was the razor shell or razor clam. They are frequently called spout fish due to their habit of ejecting a spout of water as they pull themselves rapidly down into the sand. One has to dig very quickly to catch them as they are extremely fast and seem determined to reach Australia. They are delicious, if slightly tough, when cooked.

The week could not end without fishing the pools downstream of the road bridge and the rapids. The Garden Pool was a favourite, partly because of its proximity to the house. Most fish seemed to have moved upstream and there was little activity. Memories of other years came flooding back though and of times when a number of fish came to my rod. One fish in particular will always be remembered. The river was very high and a number of fish were lying in the pool waiting to ascend when the flow moderated. Having taken three fish from the Sea Pool I came up to the Garden Pool and, fishing a size 8 Shrimp Fly, hooked a very heavy fish which moved up to the head of the pool and would not budge. Occasionally it would swim slowly towards the tail of the pool and then, keeping very deep, move back to the top of the pool. No amount of effort made any difference to it tiring. The rod being used was an old 14ft. Malloch's greenheart and it showed every sign of giving up the ghost with the pressure being exerted. Time wore on and still no sign of the fish and it never surfaced once. An hour passed and still it showed no signs of giving in. It seemed to be using the river flow to hold itself close to the bottom. After a time, knowing it was getting close to the evening meal, one of James's friends came down to see what had happened to me. He left hurriedly with a request to James to bring a net. The fish was beginning to show signs of weakening by the time James arrived, and a little stronger side strain, with the rod bending to breaking point, brought the fish to the surface. First sights can be deceptive and James remarked that it was the biggest fish he'd seen in the river. As it turned out it wasn't, but to me it felt huge. Trouble was now brewing as the fish, tiring, started to drift back to the tail of the pool and there was concern that it might drop out of the pool on the far side of the island. If this happened all would be lost. More strain was put on the rod when, with the unpredictability of greenheart, the top joint broke and slid down on to the fish's nose. Controlling the fish was now more difficult and called for desperate measures. The fish was literally hauled into the side with the top joint still wobbling over the fish's nose. Quickly James waded in and skillfully got it in the net. It weighed 14½lb., not a big fish but above average for the river. However, it was an exciting fight and helped to develop a good appetite for the evening meal now overdue and getting cold!

Greenheart was quite a pleasant material to fish with but could let one down at critical times. On another occasion a fish hooked in Harry's Run decided to return to sea and dropped down into the Nut Pool and then, with me stumbling over the rocky bank, went on down to the Sea Pool. Florence was with me at the time and was asked to net it as by now it had tired sufficiently to be brought into the side. As the net was being put in the water the spare top joint snapped and, like the previous top joint, slipped down on to the fish's nose. This time it had the expected effect and dislodged the hook. The rod had had its day and, with no more spare top joints, was retired. The insurance money went to buying a new rod, of split cane.

Our time on the Little Gruinard for this year had been full and enjoyable and one hoped that the pleasure could be repeated. Sadly, we always feel that we can carry on where we left off the year previously when it comes to arranging next year's holiday at the same place. We can never go back in time and find everything just the same. We grow older, as do our children whose interests change. The river may change; the fish stocks may alter and, in most instances, dwindle. Rivers change hands, the environment changes, unwelcome developments go ahead and, on the West Coast, salmon farms appear. If only we spent less time being in a mad rush and stopped occasionally to savour the pleasures of the moment as one might do a glass of wine. We should stop while we can and look about us, at the scenery, and listen to the song of birds and spend more time talking to our friends. Au revoir.

Chapter 3 – Days in the Dales

The sun went behind the clouds as we drove down over Oughtershaw Side into Langstrothdale. By the time we reached Hubberholme a gentle drizzle had started and on reaching Kettlewell a light rain was falling. Fortunately, we had bought our supplies in Hawes so by the time we reached our destination in Burnsall all we had to do was quickly unload the car. It rained very heavily in the night. Our cottage looked down on the River Wharfe less than 75 yards away and we could hear it from our bedroom. On drawing back the curtains in the morning the river had disappeared and in its place was a wide expanse of water covering the fields. Our neighbour came back from trying to get his Sunday papers from the village shop. The river was over the village green and up to the shop steps. He would have to wait for his papers.

Mid-day came, the sun appeared and the waters started to recede and the river gradually began to assume its normal shape. Villagers and hungry gulls busied themselves returning or, in the case of the gulls eating, the numerous crayfish which had been swept on to the Green. The important question was whether the river would be at a fishable height and colour by the following morning. We should have to wait and see.

Monday morning was dull with broken cloud but with a promise of a fine day. The river was still very high and coloured. When, as a youth, fishing the Ure at Hawes in these conditions it would have been a worm fished in all the likely eddies. Today that method was verboten. A sinking line with cast of three size 12 gold bead nymphs, a hare's ear, a dark olive and stone fly would do for a start. Half a mile downstream from the cottage there was a long pool, Hartlington Straight, below a belt of willows where the flow might be less rapid and so make fishing possible. This turned out not to be and cows in the neighbouring field came across to see what the stupid man was doing. Retracing my steps I came to a pool on a bend of the river, aptly named Cross

Bend, where the flow lessened as it widened out and produced two areas of slack water on either side of the main current. It looked particularly fishy. Casting across the current at the top of the pool the line swung round into the calm water. After a few casts the line tightened and the welcome golden gleam of a trout through the turbid water confirmed my suspicions. This was a good resting-place from the present strong flow down the river. The fish weighed 1¾lb.; the next cast produced a fish of 1½lb. from the same spot. Moving slightly down the pool, where the current had dissipated slightly, the fish were further out and two more fish were taken in quick succession, both of 1¼lb. While the next fish was being brought in the line became suddenly very much heavier and now two fish were being played! Both weighed a 1lb. One more fish was netted and, as I had three brace, was returned to the water. An autopsy of the fish revealed that they had all been gorging themselves on small crayfish and bullheads.

It was now only 11 o'clock but, as my wife and I were to attend a lunchtime talk by the Yorkshire Dales Millenium Trust at Bolton Abbey and visit a newly-planted wood, Desolation Wood, of which we were two of the many donors, it was time to reel in.

The river was still high the next day but as it was a lovely early June morning it was decided to visit an even more attractive part of the river upstream of Burnsall where access to walkers is prohibited. Again, I found the fish in the backwaters and eddies. The water was less murky and, using the same flies I cast into relatively calm water in the shade of an alder. It was not long before fish of 1¾lb, 1lb 10oz, and 1½lb were taken followed by slightly smaller fish all in the range of 1¼lb, two being taken on the same cast. A number of fish were released after reaching the bag limit. A further autopsy showed that the fish were still eating crayfish and bullheads and also worms and crane fly larvae. They would be "putting on the beef" pretty quickly if they stayed on that diet. It was soon time for lunch. The river was looking very lovely, the horse chestnuts and hawthorns were in full bloom and their reflections were mirrored in the water. It was most pleasant just to lie back and take in the view and listen to the birds – a cuckoo was calling, a Jenny wren was singing somewhere in the river bank and the willow warblers were singing in the hawthorns. We both agreed that the Yorkshire Dales take some beating.

As the week wore on the river gradually returned to a more normal summer flow. Rivers in the dales, as a result of extensive hill drainage, never remain high for any length of time. So soon there was a need for lighter casts and small dry flies. Sadly, there isn't the same amount of fly life as there used to be and it is a rare occurrence to see a proper hatch of mayflies or stoneflies. Further down the river where the little River Dibb joins the Wharfe a few trout were rising to a few flies and were beguiled by a size 14 blue quill, as was a nice grayling of 1½lb that was quickly returned. Grayling are not nearly so abundant on the Wharfe as they once were and this is true for the upper Ure as well, although there are hopeful signs of a recovery on both rivers.

When the river gets very low, dry flies like the knotted midge and black gnat dressed on size 18 and 20 hooks are needed, partly because small midges and the like are all the fly life there seems to be. I can remember 50 years ago as a boy taking trout on the neighbouring River Nidd between Pateley Bridge and Knaresborough on dry flies such as red spinner, blue upright, iron blue, steel blue and March brown dressed on hooks of sizes 12 to 16. There was rarely any need to fish with anything smaller. Then, of course, there were the huge hatches of the large green drake mayfly at the end of May and early June. These large flies have now virtually disappeared from the upper Wharfe. Dearth of fly life is a complaint on the upper Ure as well nor, sadly, is there the same quantity of fish.

Swaledale, is a more remote dale than Wensleydale, Nidderdale and Wharfedale. It is less populated, there are fewer tourists and there seems to be less traffic. Looking down the valley from Gunnerside on a summer's evening there is an air of peace with the large barns in the valley floor and a latticework of stone walls extending into the surrounding hills producing a feeling of calm. The Swale is very heavily tree-lined and this makes fly-fishing difficult. A rod of 8½ft. is all that is needed if one is to cast among the trees. The river rises very fast after heavy rain and it can be very dangerous and one must be on the lookout all the time. After one heavy flood when the river had dropped to a nice flow I worked my way up the river from Gunnerside Bridge. At one good long pool lined on one side by a row of alders the trout were rising continuously to a hatch of iron blue duns. It was just possible to wade in and, watching out for branches behind, cover the rises with a size 16 iron blue. The fly floated gently down over the lowermost fish that rose immediately and was soon on the bank. The fish were so determined that it was only a matter of time, working up the pool, before a few more fish joined the first. They were all between ten and twelve ounces and were beautifully coloured. Further upstream fish were busily rising all over a long wide pool. Access was reasonable and the ash trees were high making casting that much easier. However, it was most frustrating as every time one cast over a rise the fish stopped rising and rose further upstream. So as one moved upstream the fish, too, moved further upstream and the water that previously had rising fish appeared fishless. This was very much like the behaviour of summer grayling but, as grayling don't occur in this part of the Swale, it couldn't be grayling but simply very wary trout. Trying fishing downstream with a wet fly made no difference. So no fish came out of this pool. Some distance further upstream is a lovely round pool just below Ivelet Bridge. The left bank is heavily overgrown with trees and it is the side on which the fish tend to lie. With a bit of a struggle one can gain access to the bottom of the pool providing the river is not too high and cast upstream. Chest waders would be ideal. However, without these I managed to wade some way up the pool casting to the steadily rising fish. Two of about ¾lb. each were taken on a blue upright and then there were no further rises to the fly and other rising fish seemed to move towards the bridge and out of casting distance. The fish were very shy. The other bank of the pool was clear of trees but it was a long cast over to rising fish and, with

Springtime on the River Wharfe between Barden and Bolton Abbey

18

The River Swale at Isles Bridge, a short distance below Gunnerside.
The river is at a good height for the wet fly

the current mainly being down the left bank, there was soon drag on one's line. That was enough to deter any sensible trout from taking further interest in the fly. It is possible to cast to rising fish from the left bank above the bridge at a gap between the trees, but it is a matter of casting practically straight across and there is soon a drag on the line.

There is a comfortable seat by the bridge and next to a stone wall with its traditional style to permit an easy passage for walkers. Here one can conveniently rest with a cup of tea. It is a good spot to hear and see nuthatches. It was just above this bridge that I was surprised to see a large bat flying about in the middle of a spring afternoon. Not realising that bats came out during the day notes were exchanged with a bat expert who informed me that it would be a Daubenton's Bat. This species tends to fly during the day and likes to be by water. Any angler getting hooked up to one should be careful as this animal can carry a rabies virus.

Early September is a favourite time for us to visit Swaledale, as it is the time for the Muker Agricultural Show. This is the fitting climax to the farming year.

The dale farmers show their sheep, the farmers' wives exhibit their baking, cheese, jam, wine and knitwear. The keen local gardeners enter into competition for the best varieties of vegetables and flowers, while craftsmen, including shepherds and keepers and others enter their beautifully carved walking sticks with decorated handles. It was here that a keeper kindly sold me his stick which had the handle carved and painted in the shape of a trout and for which he'd won first prize. Throughout the day above the general hubbub the local brass band in their splendid uniforms play to an appreciative crowd. The end of and highlight of the show is the fell race. Men and young lads and lasses, sound in wind and limb, go racing across the river and up the neighbouring fell, along its top and back to the start cheered on by all.

So one can see that there is a lot more to visiting the dales than fishing for trout. Because I was brought up at the gateway to the dales and spent my fishing apprenticeship in Nidderdale and Wensleydale it is perhaps not surprising I feel this way. Most Yorkshiremen will agree!

Chapter 4 –
Horse Hair and Wensleydale Flies

It must be all of 40 years since we started using nylon in earnest for fishing. Prior to that, we religiously soaked our silkworm gut casts overnight between two damp felt pads housed in a circular aluminium cast box before use. A regular inspection for evidence of fraying of the cast was also necessary. I, for one, continued to use gut for as long as it was available because of its firmer texture guaranteeing a straighter line when it landed on the water after casting. There were no wind knots and no curly ends after tying on the fly – an irritating flaw in the early nylon. But if you have not had the pleasure of fishing with horse hair then your angling life has not been consummated. My introduction to this natural fibre came during my sojourns with the Blades family in upper Wensleydale in the 1940's.

The Blades had been anglers for four generations. The first Jimmy Blades, better known as 'Sproats', fished with nothing but horse hair. He was the local water bailiff and figures prominently in Walbran's *Grayling and How to Catch Them* and is mentioned in Bradley's *Yorkshire Anglers' Guide* of 1894. According to late T. K. Wilson, a Yorkshire angling correspondent, Jimmy Blades was probably the first to fish the dry fly on the upper Ure. The next two Jim Blades's were postmen and expert anglers and fly tiers.. The father was probably more skilful than his son, Bill Jim, and dressed flies without the aid of a vice. I remember watching him tying in the horse hair point onto the shank of an eyeless hook, so that when the fly was dressed the horse hair was secure and no amount of pulling would dislodge it. A wet fly cast was made up of strands of hair of even diameter and knotted in such a way as to allow two or three droppers to be inserted. Changing flies, stored conveniently in the parchment pockets of a leather fly wallet, was then an easy operation. To fish with such an assemblage was a dream. Agreed, the cast had to be soaked before use but, with disciplined casting, it went straight out and fished perfectly. The link between cast and fly line could be improved by having a plaited horse hair leader spliced into the end of the line. The slow action of the then commonly used greenheart rod favoured the use of horse hair. The youngest Jim, known as "Pinkie" to his friends, was an excellent angler and continued his family's fly-tying tradition. He used patterns favoured by his great grandfather, 'Sproats' Blades, especially the Red Palmer which, when tied, he gave a haircut resulting in a more effective, if not attractive, creation.

The Blades rarely purchased fly tying material but usually obtained it 'on the hoof' as it were. The fur of rabbits, hares and moles was readily available as were the feathers of grouse, partridge, pheasant, woodcock and snipe. The hackles were cultivated in the backyard on their pet bantam and Andalusian poultry. The flies were all delicately dressed and lean as a fit athlete. In my book of fly dressings I have a list of flies for each month of the season on the upper Ure. They are as follows:

March and April: Early Brown, Dark Snipe and Purple, Dark Snipe and Orange, Waterhen Bloa, Dark Spanish Needle and Checkwing. Crimson Partridge should be used in a full brown water from the beginning to the end of the season. March Brown should be used when there is a hatch of the natural fly.

May: Brown Dun Spider, Dark Woodcock and Orange, Wired Owl, Checkwing, Snipe Bloa, Dotterel Dun, Yellow-legged Bloa, Orange Partridge and Bustard.

June: Bracken Clock, Tinselled Owl, Brown Owl, Poult Bloa, Checkwing, Knotted Midge and Bustard.

July: Purple Dun, Claret Dun, Little Dun, Bracken Clock, Brown Owl and Red Palmer.

August: Purple Dun, Claret Dun, Rusty Dun, August Dun, Red Palmer and Red Ant.

September: Purple Dun, Rusty Dun, Red Palmer, Red Ant and Cinnamon Fly.

Two flies that could be usefully included are the Treacle Parkin, a good summer's evening fly, and Sturdy's Fancy. The latter, while used chiefly for grayling, can be used throughout the year and will often bring fish to the surface when there is no natural rise. It was widely used on the neighbouring River Nidd at all times of the year.

Some of the patterns figure in more than one month and, as I've found, are always reliable ones to have on one's cast. So it is perhaps of value to set out the six best dressings:

Purple Dun: *Hackle:*   Blue Andalusian cock or hen
                            Body: Purple silk dubbed with fine peacock herl
                                            and ribbed over with purple silk.

Claret Dun: *Hackle:*   Light Andalusian cock or hen
                            Body: Claret silk ribbed with fine peacock herl and
                                            ribbed over with claret silk.

Rusty Dun: *Hackle:*   Inside of young grouse wing
                            Body: Yellow silk dubbed with red fur from root of
                                            Hare's ear.

Apple Green Dun: *Hackle:*   From outside of merlin wing.
                            Body: Green silk.

Pale Autumn Dun: *Hackle:*   Light Andalusian cock or hen.
                            Body: Straw silk dubbed with heron herl.

Bracken Clock: *Hackle:*   Cock pheasant neck.
                            Body: Bronze peacock herl and red silk.

Although there has been an improvement in our fishing gear since the days of horse hair and silkworm gut, ending in the mid-1950's, the fishing environment has, alas, not followed the same path. In the 50 + years that I've fished the Ure there has been a noticeable decline in the abundance of both fly life and trout and grayling. The river had always risen and fallen rapidly, as one might expect any river to do in its upper reaches. However, the return to low water conditions occurs now almost as soon as the rain stops. The reason? Extensive land drainage schemes and overgrazing, resulting not only in low flows punctuated by flash floods, but also unstable stream beds producing inadequate spawning substrate, and increased sedimentation leading to infilling of pools and loss of fly life. There is also no doubt that agricultural chemicals, particularly synthetic pyrethroids used in sheep dip, have reduced the numbers of mayflies, stoneflies and and caddisflies. Yes, fish are still there but not in the numbers of half a century ago.

Chapter 5 – **Austria**

Petri Heil! The Austrian and German equivalent of Tight Lines was called to me as we left Michael Hofmaier at the offices of the Österreichische Fischereigesellschaft in Vienna. Michael, a fellow member of the London Flyfishers' Club, had responded to my request for information on fishing the Salza. I had planned a visit to Austria and we had arranged to stay for part of the time in Mariazell in lower Austria close to the Salza made famous by the expert French angler, Charles Ritz. Michael arranged to meet us when we reached Vienna. In true Austrian hospitality he took us out to lunch at one of those restaurants down back streets and only known to the Viennese. Our menu of dumpling soup, tafelspitz and apricot tart was truly Österreichische. After which we visited the fishery office to collect our complimentary tickets for the Salza. We would meet Michael in a few days time in Mariazell where he would accompany us on one of our days on this river renowned for good trout and grayling.

A dinky little train took us from the junction of St. Polten, a short distance from Vienna, through the mountains to Mariazell and our gasthaus the Alpenhof. A fearsome woman, who judging by the number of antlers on the walls spent much time hunting chamois and roe deer, ran this typical Austrian country inn. The weather was scorching as was the following day spent in the mountains. That is until mid-afternoon when menacing black clouds appeared and with a clap of thunder and flash of lightning a mother of all thunderstorms burst over the mountains. The effect on the river was predictable.

When we arrived at the river the following morning in bright sunshine the water was the colour of milky coffee. The chances of catching anything were pretty slim. However, we tried wet flies and a sunk line but, with the exception of one small thin brown trout, we were still fishless at lunchtime. In the hope that the water might clear sufficiently for fish to see our flies by mid-afternoon, we started to take our lunch from the car to picnic in a hayfield where hayricks

Some nice trout from the River Wharfe

were conveniently placed to make comfortable resting-places. It was not to be as, is often the nature of summer alpine weather, a thunderstorm arrived as if by magic and we had to retreat to the shelter of our car. Our chances of further fishing that day had gone.

Further heavy rain overnight ruled out fishing the next day. Michael phoned from Vienna. Yes, he had heard and sympathised but it was the nature of things in the Alps in mid-summer. In two days time he would be at his home not far from us and we were to meet him by the Erlauf, another river not far from Mariazell and, because there was a lake above where we were to fish, there was less chance of flooding.

The Erlauf at Thomauer is not as wide as the Salza. It is a rocky river with beautiful pools and gin clear water. It flows between steep fir-clad mountains. While waiting for Michael we admired from an attractive wooden bridge the numerous trout and grayling spread out across the river. The local bailiff joined us dressed in a smart grey loden suit with dark green cuffs, lapels and collar, a grey hat and the appropriate badge of office. Quite different from plus fours, tweeds and deerstalker of the traditional Scottish ghillie! After a welcome gespritze at the conveniently sited mountain inn Michael directed us to separate areas. The water was so clear one could see the fish come up to the dry fly. The weather was dull in the morning and I put up a size 16 Half Stone, a favourite fly of mine on both the Tweed and Yorkshire rivers. It was most pleasant fishing and I had a number of fish in quite a short time. All were just below the size limit of 10 inches and were returned. On a faster flowing stretch a nice grayling of 1½lb. came to a Pheasant Tail cast close to a trailing willow branch. Grayling had to be returned, as none could be taken until September. Richard had one sizeable trout which he was determined the fearsome woman at the Alpenhof would cook for him! Time passed all too quickly but Michael arranged for us to fish there again the next week, but sadly even the Erlauf was in flood by then as a result of the heavy incessant rain which is to be expected in the Alps at that time of year.

It was raining as we landed at Salzburg. Was this to be a repetition of our previous visit? The first couple of days in Bad Aussee in the Styrian Salzkammergut would suggest it was. However, the sun came out, the mist

The Ödenseer Traun near Kainisch

A beautiful trout from the Ödenseer Traun

and clouds lifted to reveal a spectacular backcloth of steep mountains looking down on us. I had already made contact with the head Forester by letter and all was arranged to fish the Ödenseer Traun at Kainisch. Fischmeister Gustav Öhlinger, who ran a fish farm rearing Brook Trout for the table, rented from the Austrian Forest Service 6 kilometres of this river. He also had a splendid Forellen Stüberl where one could have trout or lake herring, sometimes known as whitefish. The Traun was a pretty little river with very clear water. Herr Öhlinger made it clear that all fish we caught must be on dry fly and were to be returned to the river. He obviously wanted us to eat in his Forellen Stüberl. Most Austrian rivers impose a very strict bag limit of one or two fish. This is made clear on fishing notices or tickets with the words: Fanglimit 2 Stück (i.e. 2 fish). Some, like Herr Öhlinger require all fish to be returned. Richard and I were not deterred and on a beautiful morning we started catching and returning fish at a very pleasing rate. The fish were not choosy about flies but Red Quill, Tup's Indispensable and Treacle Parkin were popular. We never knew which of the three species of fish we would hook next – brown trout (Bachforelle), rainbow trout (Regenbogenforelle) or brook trout (Bachsaibling). The fish weighed between 8oz to 12 oz. The only fish we didn't catch was the grayling (Äsche). Probably because of the crystal-clear water the colours of the fish were superb. The brook trout colouration was magical and the brown trout had the most vivid red spots encircled in white.

Herr Ruppe, mine host of our Blau Traube gasthaus, feeling sorry for us when we said that we had to return all the fish we caught, bought some trout from a neighbouring trout farm for our dinner. It made a change from the ever-present dumplings on the menu. Dumplings are called knödel. We had goose, veal, beef all mit knödel! So to relieve the monotony we were frequent visitors to Herr Öhlinger's Forellen Stüberl. Frau Öhlinger was an expert fish cook and had a nationwide reputation for her recipes. These included rainbow trout with almonds, mushrooms, garlic, cream sauce, pepper sauce as well as Forelle blau (blue trout) and Forelle blau with a delicious red wine sauce. Brook trout (Saibling) and whitefish (reinanken or rehnke), which we know as Powan, were also served. One could start one's meal with a smoked trout fillet soup, Herr Öhlinger had a smoke house below the restaurant, and finish with bilberries whipped up in delicious vanilla ice cream. There was also a very

Bachsaibling (brook trout) taken from the Traun. The colouration is quite striking.

29

good house white wine – Strasser Grüner Veltliner. The fish-eating habits of Austrians and Germans are quite characteristic to them. For example, it is quite common to see the local gasthofs advertising *Fischspezialitatabend* (Fish speciality evening) with candlelight and folk music, and trout is prominent on most menus.

A small tributary of the Ödenseer Traun is the Krunglbach, which I fished on another occasion while staying at the schloss of Herr Frei, the head forester near Bad Mittendorf. These smaller streams, referred to as –bach, are best fished after rain! So one usually had plenty of opportunity to fish them. The Krunglbach was a productive little stream and a delightful water to fish unlike the Tauernbach near Mallnitz, which I fished on one occasion. It was too torrential with few resting-places for fish. The proprietor had bulldozed channels to try and form pools but the next spate from snow melt in the neighbouring mountains washed all his efforts away. I had just three very thin trout.

Austria is a beautiful country in which to fish particularly in the more mountainous areas where the alpine flowers and scenery are a joy. However, one must expect disappointments, as in the summer the river levels are governed by frequency of thunderstorms and, in hot weather, by snowmelt from the mountains. Auf Wiedersehen!

Chapter 6 – Mývatn

It was while Tumi Tómasson of the Institute of Freshwater Fisheries in Reykjavik was working with me at Edinburgh University that the subject of big brown trout in Iceland came up. Yes, undoubtedly the best brown trout river in Iceland was the upper Laxá í Adaladalur. There are a number of Icelandic rivers called Laxá, lax being the Norse name for salmon, but this one is probably the largest and runs out of the lake Mývatn in the north-east of the country and flows north to enter the Arctic Ocean near Husavik. Mývatn is Icelandic for midge (mý means midge and vatn lake). The upper river is inaccessible to salmon. The trout fishing is so much in demand that it is booked up by the beginning of each year. Yes, he could get me tickets.

Our flight had been delayed in Glasgow. It seemed there was no aircraft and one had to be flown from somewhere in Europe. All passengers were sent across to the airport hotel for dinner. We sat next to Iceland's strongest man who was returning home from the World's Strongest Man Competition. He was a pleasant man and, perhaps surprisingly, not a big eater. The aircraft eventually arrived. Judging by its interior it had only just been converted from carrying cargo and was uncomfortable. We landed at Keflavik at some unearthly hour in the morning and, as it was the end of June, it was light here the full 24 hours. The security on arrival was tight and worse than at departure as some European monarch was due. The airport bus finally left for Reykjavik. We were all tired and all we wanted was bed. It must have been nearly four when we reached our hotel room. We had to be up early to catch a flight to Akureyri.

The alarm went all too soon. Richard's eyes were bleary through lack of sleep and it was an effort to get moving. Judging by the appearance of other passengers for the early flight from the city airport we weren't the only ones who had found it difficult to wake up. Public transport was supposed to be

A 3¼lb. brown trout taken on a Peter Ross from the Laxá below Mývatn

available at Akureyri to take us to Hótel Reynihlíd at Mývatn. Not surprisingly there wasn't any, so we joined the tour bus and had a guided journey north stopping at Godafoss Falls en route.

The first views of the river came up to all my expectations. It is wide and fast flowing with a fairly steep gradient. The rapids alternate with long pools interspersed with islands with luxuriant vegetation of willows, angelica and marsh marigolds providing backwaters and eddies giving shelter to trout and duck. The stony bed provides an ideal substrate for water creatures particularly the larvae of black flies which carpet the stones in their thousands and provide ample food for ducks, phalaropes and – trout!

An essential part of one's fishing equipment is a head net rather like a beekeeper's net. Midge lake is not called this for nothing. These midges are not related to the minute Scottish midge that bites but are very much larger and do not bite. However, they hatch in their billions and the swarms look like columns of black smoke. They cluster all round you and become quite unbearable. I've seen anglers having to leave the river because they had no head net. In addition there are the black flies which are not quite so numerous but do bite. They delight in taking chunks out of you. They are most prevalent in damp calm weather.

Our first day's fishing was the lowest beat on the stretch for which we had tickets and is called Brettingstadir. We reached it in our hire car via a rough track running through interesting terrain. The first pool was Strengir and here we had our first three trout which, with the aid of the fast current, fought hard even though they were relatively small at an average size of 1½lb. All were taken on a size 8 Peter Ross. There were favourite flies for the river and Peter Ross was one of them. Others were Black Ghost, Holmfridur, Royal Coachman and thingeyingur. All, except Peter Ross, were dressed on long shank hooks and closely resembled streamer flies.

I wondered whether we were fishing deep enough. Every so often I was getting light plucks on my line and the reason was soon revealed when my line

Arctic terns looking for insects over the Laxá. Sometimes the insects are the angler's flies, so beware

The tame little red-necked phalarope is quite oblivious to anglers and is quite likely to swim around you while you're fishing.

took to the air with an arctic tern attached to the other end! It was eventually grounded and covered with my hat. Fortunately the line was only round one wing and it was soon released. We needed to fish deeper.

After lunch taken by a fishing hut and sitting in a breeze to keep the midges away, a move was made down to Vordufidi, a long deep and very wide pool. Two anglers on the other side were in neoprene waders and up to their waists in the water and periodically catching nice fish. I soon had a real tug and played a hard fighting trout, which eventually succumbed. It was a more presentable weight of 3¼lb. and a beautiful fish very heavily spotted. We had no more fish that day. We agreed that we needed to be fishing deeper and faster sinking lines were needed, at least on that part of the river.

We had only a half-day's fishing permit the next day so some bird photography was in order. The area is an incredible haven for birds, particularly waterfowl. Harlequin and Barrow's Goldeneye are mostly seen on the river along with the friendly little Red-necked Phalaropes which practically swim in between your legs. The lake is the home of a huge variety of ducks that can be seen in rafts or flocks in sheltered bays. Scaup, wigeon, tufted duck, long-tailed duck, teal, pintail, shoveler and common scoter all breed here, as do Slavonian grebe and red-throated divers. In the surrounding area there are golden plover, dunlin, whimbrel and ptarmigan and the ubiquitous redshank that follow you everywhere uttering their piping alarm call incessantly.

Evidence of the volcanic nature of the country was to be seen everywhere. Fields of lava came right down to Reynihlid and the neighbouring church and pseudo craters were to be seen near the lake. Hot springs were only a short distance east and the recently active volcanic fissure, Krafla, was only a ten-minute drive away.

Our next day was on Arnarvatn with pools above and below the main road bridge. A head-net was essential today, particularly to keep away the black flies. Quite a few more fish of between 1¼ and 1½lb came to the net. Most of these were taken on a size 6 thingeyingur and size 8 Peter Ross. The best fish of the day weighed 3½lb and was caught in Brautarstensvad, situated above a wooden bridge leading to the island of Geldingaey. Although we had had reasonable sport we both felt that the use of a heavier and faster sinking line

The harlequin drake and duck have quite striking colouration. Iceland is the only European country they frequent.

35

would have produced more fish. This would have applied in the case of a deep pool, which widened out into the size of a very small lake where two branches of the river joined at Nýavad. We suspected that the fish lay down at the bottom of a sloping shelf where the two branches joined. A shop near the hotel had one fast sinking line so we put this on one of our reels and it had a beneficial effect, although the water we fished on our last day was not as deep as some parts of the river we'd fished earlier in the week. Our last day was at Geirastadir which lies closer to Mývatn. This is an attractive stretch, fairly shallow and fast flowing with small pools making ideal fish resting places. At the bottom of the pool Helgeyjarsker was a willow-covered island with deep holes on either side. Casting across the river my line with its size 8 Royal Coachman swung round and hovered in front of the island. Something very heavy attached itself to the line and all we could see was a dark shadow weaving around the pool in the sunlight. The fish was eventually persuaded to come into the bank and was led in to a small inlet where Richard was just ready to net it when everything went slack. These things happen! Not to be discouraged the same place was fished over again and this time a fish of 2½lb was successfully landed.

Well, it had been a wonderful week in most unique surroundings. We had caught some beautiful trout and seen a variety of birds including some that we don't see in Scotland. There would be a lot to tell Tumi on our return home.

Chapter 7 – **The Long Haul-in**

A little tired of catching brown trout of hatchery origin and alien rainbow trout which now seem to dominate angling waters in Central Scotland and elsewhere, I decided to take my son to a place where wild fish still abound. Iceland, a country Burton referred to as Ultima Thule, tends to 'grow on you' and is probably the reason for regular visits over the last decade or so.

Icelanders will tell you that if the weather is fine in the south around Reykjavik it will be wet in the north of the island and vice versa. Fortunately, for those anglers who prefer to fish closer to the Arctic Circle, it is usually much finer in the north, particularly in the north-east which lies in the rain shadow of Vatnajökull, the largest glacier in Europe. Consoled by this information, we happily left Reykjavik early one very wet morning in the knowledge that when we reached Midfördur the sun would be shining.

In late June it never gets dark at this latitude and the sun had been streaming through the thin curtains of our room from a very early hour. Judging by the activity on the farm it would appear that some folk never go to bed at this season. We were therefore not surprised to find our guide, Gudjon, waiting while we breakfasted on skyr, smoked herring and cheese.

On the map, Kvislarvatn did not seem too far from our farm at Brekkulaekur, and from where we were to leave the four-wheel drive vehicle the lake seemed only a ten-minute stroll away. Maps can be deceptive! After a spine-jerking forty-five minute drive along an uneven track by the Midfjaradara, Gudjon assured us we were nearly there. It was just a matter of a slight climb and a fifteen-minute walk across the Arnavatnsheidi moors. Armed with such reassuring knowledge Fritz, our German companion, a well-built butcher from Dortmund, pulled on his thigh waders while I shouldered a camera tripod and a rucksack. The light rucksack on my son Richard's back and a twinkle in his eye indicated that the young are not always unwise.

A flock of Whooper swans grazing nearby was as good an excuse as any to stop to catch one's breath after a twenty minute uphill walk between knee-height mounds of grass-covered earth spaced irregularly across the terrain and designed to make the walk twice as long. Where was the lake? A distant hill was pointed out. Our goal was just the other side of that, only another twenty minutes. My sweater followed my Grenville jacket into the rucksack. Fritz's waders were still at mast height.

Six Great Northern Divers sailed gracefully away from the lake shore as we hove into sight. Before the tripod could be set up and the telephoto lens brought to bear on these lovely birds, Gudjon let out a yell, "A bloody mink!" and shot off in hot pursuit. An imitation of a wounded animal halted the mink in its tracks momentarily but before the pursuer could strike the quarry had reached its den. The divers were not amused and had drifted to the centre of the lake.

A cold north wind was blowing from a cloudless sky and no fish were rising. So it was a sinking line with size 10 Blae and Black, Peter Ross and Alexandra. Deep water near the cabin for overnight stays soon yielded a nice 1½lb trout to Richard. Yes, but there are much bigger trout Gudjon assured us and demonstrated the veracity of his statement by hauling out two of over 2lb a piece on something that looked suspiciously like a Red Dog Nobbler, shades of reservoir fishing for rainbows!

Heavily weighted flies on a sinking line seemed necessary, although charr of half a pound or so took close to the surface. The Alexandra was the most rewarding fly, we had all left our Dog Nobblers at home. Very large brownies were not in evidence although something stopped Richard's line and, as he put it: "It was though someone had attached a concrete block to the line and let it fall". Alas, the cast broke. Sport eventually eased up and, rather than stay the "night", we made a gradual downhill descent by a quicker but longer and more attractive route through terrain liberally covered with alpine flowers. On this return walk our suspicions that our guide was a natural hunter were confirmed. As a raven alighted on a crag, Gudjon emitted a 'craaaak', which triggered an immediate response from the raven, which left its perch and came over to look for an intruding member of its species. For the next few minutes there was a duologue between the raven and Gudjon which was only broken off when we suggested that if his conversation with the fish was as impressive we should continue to do well! The response to that remark was that to hear a raven croak would bring good luck.

Torfustadavatn was nearer base and to reach it involved only a short drive and a gentle uphill walk. Not only was the lake full of fish but the bird life was prolific. Long-tailed duck and scaup were to be seen in the sheltered bays and the odd whooper swan and great northern diver appeared from time to time. An incursion into the surrounding moor would guarantee attention from fussy whimbrels, redshank and golden plover, with an occasional interjection from black-tailed godwits. With mounds of moss campion and carpets of mountain avens, known locally as the ptarmigan plant, and mountain azalea growing in profusion what more could one want?

We soon found that the fish were not in the middle of the lake, as one always supposes, but very close to the shore. Under the perfect weather conditions we experienced odd rises could be spotted. At first, because the rises were in very shallow water, it was thought they were small fish. However, by wading close in to the side and casting parallel to the bank sizeable fish took as one's flies alighted on the water. If it was a charr it took off for the middle of the lake and bored deeply, hardly if ever breaking the surface. The trout were more active fighters but tired quicker. We guessed the reason for the fish being close to the shore was their waiting for morsels to be blown off the land by the ever-present north wind. The Alexandra, Black Pennell and Butcher were the most successful flies but for most of the time we fished just with the Alexandra which imitated the three-spined stickleback which was present in large numbers.

Fritz landed the biggest charr at just over 2lb. If this lake had a fault it was one which occurs in many shallow Iceland lakes. If there is a very strong wind the bottom silt is stirred up and remains in suspension for some time, making the water yellow and opaque for a day or so after the wind has lessened.

R.N. Stewart in his book *Rivers of Iceland* refers to the brown trout in the large sea lagoon called Lake Hop as being numerous and reaching a large size, fish of 8lb being nothing unusual. Trout of any size were conspicuous by their absence when we visited the lake that is so large that bank fishing, even when one's guide knows the area, is something of a gamble. The few charr that we connected with were lanky and pale mauve in colour and nothing like their brilliantly coloured counterparts from the moorland lakes on Arnavatnsheidi. The presence of parasites on their tongues and gills suggested that they were sea-run charr kelts. However, probably later in the year the lake is more rewarding and the presence of metres of discarded nylon and bait hooks would suggest that it was a popular venue for local anglers at some time! This was the only place visited in Iceland where anglers' litter was obvious.

As one can fish for salmon in this water the daily close-time from 14.00 to16.00 hours is enforced. We became aware of this when an official-looking helicopter hovered above us for a while shortly after the commencement of the compulsory break to ensure that we were not fishing. It was reassuring to know that the authorities can enforce these measures in such a sparsely populated country.

Lake Hop area is rewarding in other ways, and the sighting of eight drake harlequins where the Vididalsa enters the lake and our car being parked in the middle of a snow bunting's territory were sufficient recompense for a day's fishing. The beauty of the trout and charr fishing in Iceland is that, although one can take a four-wheeled drive vehicle some of the way to one's destination, the final part of the journey has to be made on foot. It is this long haul-in, with all its association with nature, which one member of our Royal family referred to as being such an important part of the fishing experience which we are tending to lose sight of nowadays. So often the success of a fishing trip is measured in numbers of fish caught rather than enjoyment of the wilderness experience. Let us hope we are wise enough to preserve this wilderness.

Chapter 8 – The Quest for Bleikja

Having spent expensive days in Iceland fishing for salmon on the Grimsá and Nordurá and much more exciting times fishing for charr in that country, I tend to agree with the late Major-General R.N. Stewart who says in his book *Rivers of Iceland* that: "Any angler could spend a holiday in Iceland if content with charr fishing for very much less expenditure than if he demanded salmon fishing." Stewart was, of course, referring to fishing for migratory charr which enter the rivers in the north of the country from July onwards.

Many of the larger rivers holding these migratory charr, or Bleikja as they are known in Icelandic, are first and foremost salmon rivers and for that reason are nor always available to the charr angler until the salmon season is over. However, some of the smaller northern rivers, because their water temperatures are too low for salmon, are predominantly charr waters and are more accessible to the itinerant angler going on spec.

So, early August found David Piggins and I winging north from Reykjavik in a Norlandair five-passenger aircraft. David was concerned at the absence of a co-pilot and kept passing fruit pastilles at regular intervals to the pilot in the hope that he wouldn't have a heart attack and plummet us into the unfriendly mountains below. I pointed out that his fruit pastilles were more likely to choke him than his having a heart attack. The flight was uneventful but fascinating as one attempted to identify some of the world-famous salmon rivers such as the Laxá í Kjos, Vatnsdalsa and Midfjaradara. A rather unnerving hedgehop over a power line stretched 20 feet above one end of the short runway announced our arrival at Olafsfjordur.

The Olafsfjardara is a very small river flowing from a mountainous region hemming in the little village of Olafsfjordur between it and the sea, with no land between it and the small arctic island of Grimsey. At the lower end of the

Richard playing a large trout on Kvislarvatn

river is Olafsfjorduravatn. This is a most unusual lake classified by limnologists as being meromictic, that is a lake that has an upper layer of fresh water and a lower one of salt water due to the intrusion of the sea at high tide. For those scientifically minded one might also add that in addition to having a thermocline (a horizontal boundary layer at a certain depth at which there is a marked change in temperature) as do most deep bodies of water in the summer, it has an oxycline (at which there is a change in oxygen) and a halocline (where there is a change in salinity). So, not only can freshwater fish species such as charr be caught in the lake but also marine forms like cod and herring. These phenomena were of value to a salmon farm that was sited on the lake shore, as it allowed warm (15°C) saline water to be pumped to its fish tanks from below the halocline throughout the year even when there was total ice cover on the lake. The hatchery tanks therefore had a good supply of sea water as well as a source of cool spring water from the neighbouring mountains

The river, which only holds charr, is divided into two beats with a change-over for rods at about mid-day. We had the upper beat and, as rain some days before had brought the first run of charr in from the sea, we were optimistic. Our optimism was justified and we soon had some fresh-run fish as bright as new 10p pieces on the bank. The tactics were to fish a sink-tip line diagonally down and across the river using standard casts of largish flies (sizes 10 and 12) such as Teal, Blue and Silver, Black Pennell and Blae and Silver, and then to retrieve slowly, raising the rod as the flies were brought round with the current. The fish took gently but firmly and there was no messing about with splashy short rises. The fish meant business every time and, as Stewart says: "There is little difficulty in catching charr; of all fishes I know they are the most ready takers." Once hooked they take off in no uncertain manner and stay deep and pull very hard without the intermittent acrobatics displayed by other members of the salmonidae. Even when fishing in Icelandic lakes one could always tell when one had hooked a charr as they are much better fighters than trout. However, when they 'go off the take', and it can happen quite suddenly, nothing will tempt them to rise. It is as if there wasn't a fish in the river. One minute you are rising and playing fish and the next it's gone completely dead.

We enjoyed excellent sport for the two days we had on the Olafsfjardara. The fish were not large, none over 2lb., although we were told much larger fish used to be caught. The reason for the change was probably due to a salmon

Bringing in a sea-run charr on the Olafsfjardara

43

Sea-run charr fresh in from the sea

ranching scheme at the mouth of the river run in conjunction with the salmon farm. The owners had built a trap and fence across the mouth of the river and only the smaller charr could pass through the vertical bars of the fence screens, the larger fish ended up with the salmon in the trap and were not passed upstream. Fortunately, there have been changes to this procedure.

The Eyjafjardara is in the third division of Icelandic salmon rivers but is good for migratory charr. The river rises in the bleak central mountain range and flows into Eyjafordur a mile or so east of Iceland's northern capital, Akureyri. This was our base while fishing the Eyjafjardara and two neighbouring rivers, the Fnöská and Hörgá.

The Eyjafjardara had already had a rise in water a couple of weeks earlier and consequently many of the charr had moved well upstream. Luckily, a local angler pointed out the pools in which they were likely to be found. The fish we caught were mostly in excess of 2lb. and came to the flies used on the Olafsfjardara and also to the Crosfield (a good Icelandic salmon fly), Badger and Silver and Stoat's Tail. The colour of the fish in this river was spectacular. Most, having been in fresh water for a while, were no longer silver but had developed a technicolour dreamcoat. Some had steel-grey backs and red bellies with flanks liberally covered with pink spots. Their black pectoral and anal fins had pure white margins. Others had green flanks, covered with straw-coloured spots, and pink bellies. These most desirable fish had no intentions of being landed easily when hooked and gave us plenty of exercise chasing downstream after them. Most fought like salmon twice their size and one could be forgiven thinking at first that one had hooked a reasonable-sized grilse. We could have spent more than two days fishing and exploring this river but a day had been arranged for us on the Fnjöska.

The Fnjöska, to the north of Akureyri, is another third division salmon river and our visit as far as charr were concerned, was fruitless. We were told by friends at the Institute of Freshwater Fisheries in Reykjavik that the charr would have been many miles upstream of the beats we were allocated. However, the river runs through a beautiful valley bordered by steep mountains with snow on the more sheltered slopes glistening in the sun, and the only thing to mar the day was the absence of food and drink. We had come without sandwiches as we had noticed on the map the neighbouring community of Grenivik where we thought we could get something to eat. On arrival at the village during the statutorily

A 2¼lb. sea-run arctic charr from the Eyjafjaradara in spawning livery

45

enforced lunch break imposed by fishery regulations we found the place deserted. In the one store-cum-café chairs were stacked on top of tables and everything was locked up, not a soul to be seen. We then drove frantically a short distance to a small country museum at Laufas. Yes, we could look around, at a price, no, they did not sell refreshments. Even David's considerable charm could not wheedle coffee out of the guide, whose house was nearby. Icelanders can be as dour as Highlanders at times. So we resorted to handfuls of bilberries growing in profusion by the riverside to temporarily quench our thirst and alleviate the pangs of hunger until our return to civilization.

Rivers originating from glaciers and snowfields are very cold and greyish white in colour, reminiscent of pulp mill effluent. Consequently they are not conducive to successful fly-fishing as we found when we turned up at the Hörgá just west of Akureyri. It's too cold for salmon but suits the charr and also some sea trout apparently, as a small one came to the small blue and silver MEPS spoon to which we had to resort. We took some handsome silver charr on this lure as they swam in from the sea a hundred or so metres downstream of us. Interestingly, some of the large glacial rivers in south-eastern Iceland hold good runs of large sea trout but no salmon. On the other hand there are some glacial rivers in the south-west, such as the Hvitá and Thjorsá, which have very good runs of salmon. We agreed that it would be well worth fishing the Hörgá with fly when there had been no rain on the glaciers to turn the otherwise clear waters grey, a condition that doesn't happen very often. However, it was an interesting experience, especially to see the charr come right up to the surface to literally swallow the MEPS as it was being taken out of the water at the end of a retrieve.

On our flight south in a more substantial aircraft than that which had brought us north, we agreed that, while it had been a successful venture fishwise, what had made it particularly special was the scenery and wildlife. There are the everlasting memories of the shrill cries of the gyr falcons wheeling overhead, the plaintive piping of the golden plovers and the pinkfeet geese grazing unconcernedly by the riverside. The plants, too, were magnificent in their modest way and lured David into botanical forays whenever sport slackened. There were the delicate yellow Arctic poppies growing in clusters in the river gravel and the purple Arctic river beauty, closely related to our much taller rosebay willowherb, growing in masses of deep pink on the gravel banks by the river. Presiding over all were the mountains conjuring up mental images of the myths of Tolkien. Yes, we would come back.

Chapter 9 – The Exploits of a Scots Angler, James Maitland Burnett

It is not often one comes across old fishing logbooks, so it was exciting to be lent the fishing register and diaries of a James Maitland Burnett. All the more exciting because they contained valuable records of salmon fishing in Iceland at the end of the nineteenth century before few if any Icelanders engaged in the sport. It was mainly Englishmen who came to the country to fish, Rider Haggard, author of *King Solomon's Mines*, being such a one.

Burnett was born in 1844 at Barns near Peebles and was the last male representative of the Burnets of Barns made famous through the novel *John Burnet of Barns* by John Buchan. Burnett was a man of considerable attainments, being a great linguist, an authority on the Flemish language and for some time Honorary Secretary and Treasurer of the Royal Philatelic Society of London. He was also a member of the select Tweeddale Shooting Club.

His diaries describing his visits to Iceland start in 1883. In that year he sailed from Granton on 14th June on the *Camorus*. He reached the Westmann Islands on the 18th and disembarked at Reykjavík a day later. The first fortnight of his stay was spent travelling. He set out from Reykjavik on 21st June with 22 ponies and reached Mossfell after crossing the forbidding Mt. Esja to the north of the town. Accommodation was limited and he and his friend, Walter Trevelyan, slept in their coats at either side of the altar in the local church. The next day saw them in Theril after changing horses at the Laxá at Reynivellir and waiting for the tide to recede sufficiently to allow them to cross Hvalfjord. A fjord now negotiable at all states of tide via a tunnel. They reached Reykholt on 23rd June after stopping at Leirá for lunch. They were not hospitably received by the parson at Reykholt and had only coffee and rusks for dinner.

On their journey to Gilsbakki the following day they had an arduous crossing of the Hvita which the ponies had to swim. When they reached the parsonage at Gilsbakki they were more warmly received by the local priest who gave them coffee and salted char for dinner and allowed them to fish.

Burnett and his companion found the fishing in this area very disappointing. The terrain made it difficult to reach the distant lakes they had planned to fish and they decided to return south on 29th June. They recrossed the Hvitá and Reykjadalsa in which there were springs of boiling water. Finally, after fording the Grimsa and experiencing some heavy climbing, they reached Skorraldalsvatn. They crossed the end of this lake that Burnett said contained no fish owing, it was thought, to its being inhabited by a water monster. They reached Theril very early in the morning after a 16-hour ride. Two days later the party reached their destination at Wassendi and, after setting up their tents by the Dimá which is the upper reach of the Ellidaár from Ellidavatn downstream to a point where the inflow of a major tributary changes the river's name to Ellidaár.

Some of the Dimá is now submerged due to the damming of the river by a hydro-electric project, which has increased the size of Ellidavatn. Now the outskirts of a rapidly expanding Reykjavík look down on a river whose flow is regrettably controlled by man.

The fishing was rented from Olafr, the farmer, for Kr.80. This payment was also to include payment to the farmer who owned the lower pool on the river. Burnett seemed to guard his newly acquired rights to the fishing zealously and on occasions he had to warn off a regular poacher by the name of Weinholt. Things got to such a stage that one of the farmers marched Weinholt's ponies across the river.

Burnett's remarks were: *'W. was profane – we shall see what comes of it.'* The fishing this year was not exceptionally good and the best day's catch were 15 salmon and 4 grilse, followed by a day with 8 salmon and 9 grilse. Extremely good by anyone's standards nowadays! For some unknown reason more time was spent trout fishing than in later years, when the greater part of every day was occupied catching salmon. This may have been partly due to his spending time arranging a longer and more permanent lease for future years and making social visits locally. River netting at the river mouth by a certain gentleman named Thomson might have been another explanation. However, a great deal of time was spent trout fishing on the Hólmsá and Laeká (this is probably the stream Skyggnislaekur, an unpronounceable name for a foreigner!) as well as on the Dimá. Daily catches of trout on occasions amounted to as many as 40 or 50 fish, and on one day, on the Dimá, 70 fish – on worm.

Arrangements for a long lease on the Dimá were tedious –

25th August – "In the evening had a talk with Olafr who agreed to let the river for 6 years at Kr.250 per annum."

26th August – "In the evening Olafr came to discuss the terms of our contract but after talking for hours matters were not advanced."

27th August – "In the evening went into Reykjavík with Thordur and Olafr to discuss the terms of our lease. After a wearisome discussion of 3 hours 0. Signed."

A little earlier in the month Burnett had arranged to pay Jón Jónsson, the farmer who owned the lower pools Kr.45 per annum for 6 years.

28th August – "called on Jón Jónsson and got him to sign his agreement….In the evening sent Thordur to Hafnafjord to deposit the agreement with the Sysselman." - *(Sysselman is a magistrate).*

This fishing agreement is probably the oldest on record in Iceland and is worth setting out in full:

I, the undersigned, do hereby bind myself and heirs to let Messrs. Maitland Burnett and Walter Trevelyan, jointly and severally, my fishing rights in the rivers… For six years from the 1st January, 1884. The following to be the conditions of the contract:

1. Messrs. Burnett and Trevelyan are to pay me, or my heirs the sum of……kroner yearly.

2. Payment to be made every year, one half of ….kr on or before 1st July and the other half of…..kr not later than September 1st.

3. *The money to be paid whether Messrs. Burnett and Trevelyan come to Iceland or not.*

4. *Should Messrs. Burnett and Trevelyan not come to Iceland, they may give the right of fishing to one or more friends.*

5. *Whether Messrs. Burnett and Trevelyan come to Iceland or not, I bind myself not to give to any one save to their friends, permission to fish nor will I fish myself with either rod, net or any other instrument.*

6. *I also bind myself to protect by law the sole right of Messrs. Burnett and Trevelyan to fish in my waters during the specified time and to prosecute any person, or persons, on fringing the rights which I hereby grant to Messrs. Burnett and Trevelyan.*

7. *If at any time before the expiry of this lease, Mr. Thomsen should succeed in establishing the right which he claims to the sole right of fishing in these rivers, or should Messrs. Burnett and Trevelyan be disturbed in fishing through any cause which it is in my power to prevent then this contract shall be void for the year in which such disturbance or interruption occurs unless the cause of dispute shall be arranged by two arbitrators, one to be chosen by me and one by Messrs. Burnett and Trevelyan.*

8. *All the salmon and trout caught by Messrs. Burnett and Trevelyan are to be their property.*

9. *Should I remove from the farm before the end of these six years and should I not be able to procure for Messrs. Burnett and Trevelyan the right which I hereby grant to them upon the same conditions from my successor to the farm then this contract shall be void.*
(The above paragraph was inserted for Jón Jónsson)

We, the undersigned, hereby bind ourselves to carry out all these clauses of the above contract.

Paragraph 7 is interesting and it must have given Burnett some satisfaction and delight when, on 29th July, after returning from the christening of his god-daughter, Thordur's child, he noticed people from Reykjavík setting up a tent near Thomsen's river (i.e. the Ellidaár) and holding a jollification to celebrate his defeat in a salmon trap case.

More about this chap Thomsen. There had been a dispute between Thomsen and Benedikt Sveinsson, owner of Ellidavatn and father of the great Icelandic poet, Einar Benediktsson. Later Thomsen sold the Ellidaár to an Englishman, a Mr. Payne, whom subsequently sold the river to the town of Reykjavík.

The 1883 fishing season ended for Burnett with a total of 75 salmon, 103 grilse, 23 sea trout and 598 brown trout. His future lease of the Dimà appeared secure and he had made many friends and been made a godparent. He gave an account of the christening of his godchild:

I went to Thordur's house where the family was assembled. Soon afterwards the priest appeared and the baby was brought in. The ceremony opened with a dismal kind of hymn and then the priest seemed to conduct the rest of the service extemporarily. The child's head was held over a slop basin and the priest filled his hand 3 times with water and poured it over his head. The name given was Björg Maitland. After the baptism came a collation. First each guest was served a cup of chocolate, then with a cup of coffee and finally with a gruesome liquid of white port wine (probably Brennadin or Schnapps). *Almost a dozen different cakes and biscuits were handed out and we all drank the health of the babe and the parents.*

The start of Burnett's visit to Iceland the next year almost ended in tragedy. After leaving Granton on 5th July on the *Camorus* in thick fog the passengers experienced a slow passage north on account of the reduced visibility. Then at 6 p.m. on 6th July when everyone was sitting down to dinner the ship ran aground in the Pentland Firth. Luckily no one was lost and, after some days delay on the grounded ship, Burnett transferred to the *Craigforth* on 14th July and sailed for Reykjavík in the evening. After a wretched voyage in high seas Reykjavík was reached on 18th July.

There seemed to be some last minute hitch in his fishing agreement with Olafr as, on the day of his arrival, he remarks: 'Wrote letter in answer to one from Olafr intimating our terms and telling him to accept them or leave them.' All seems to have been settled as his diary soon becomes a list of fish caught. On 28th July he refers to a meeting with the Stirlings who rode over to see him while waiting for a passage home. They had been fishing the Langa and had killed 370 fish.

Burnett records two fortnightly payments to Olafr on this visit. One of Kr.112 on 5th August and one of Kr.123 on 18th August. He appeared to have an agreement to fish the Ellidavatn, the lake at the head of the Dimá, at this time as well, as on 28th August his diary entry reads:

Thordur rode to Ellidavatn early in the morning with agreement for Saemundar to sign and Kr.50 for this year's fishing.

His salmon catches this year were well up on those for 1883. He had four outstanding days with bags of 14, 13, 13 and 12 salmon respectively. His total catch for 31 days fishing was 169 salmon and grilse weighing 865lbs. and 175 sea trout, brown trout and char weighing 184lbs. The average weight of salmon was 5lb.

The final entry in his fishing register for 1884 read:

This was the worst summer known in Iceland for 20 years. From the middle of July to the time I left (3rd September) the rain was almost incessant and the gales heavy. The river was constantly over its banks and the water discoloured. For several days fishing was impossible. There was a good deal of distress in the Island owing to the failure of the cod fishing and the loss of the hay crop owing to the bad weather.

There is no diary for the years 1885 to 1887, but fortunately Burnett wrote fairly extensive notes in his fishing register for these three years. 1885 was not a productive year with no more than 9 salmon being taken on any one day, although occasional good bags of up to 58 trout were recorded. The most popular flies seem to have been Alexandra, Butcher, Popham, Jock Scott and Silver Doctor. During flood conditions a Phantom Devon or Spoon was used.

The total for 30 days fishing in 1885 was 106 salmon and grilse – 679lbs. and 313 trout – 356lbs. The average weight of salmon was a little over 6½lbs.The last entry for this year reads:

'The worst fishing I have had in Iceland.'

The next season was as spectacular a success as 1885 was a failure. There were several days on which salmon catches ran into double figures. For example, from July 20th to August 5th the daily salmon totals were: 17, 13, 18, 10, 25, 24, 37, 28, 19, 18, 14, 18, 26, 15, 18, 17 and 17! A number of other fly patterns appear in the register this year including Childers, Eagle Thigh, Grey Eagle, Lion, Summer Duck, Thunder and Lightning and Wilkinson.

The 54-day catch for 1886 amounted to 599 salmon and grilse – 3917lbs. and 531 trout – 572lbs. The largest salmon weighed 15lbs.

The 1887 season was the last in which catches were entered in the Register and there is no evidence from the Remarks column that there is anything fundamentally wrong. Burnett did have an interview with Saemundar a few days after his arrival, but there is no indication that the earlier fishing agreement on Ellidavatn was being disputed. At the end of July he caught a poacher and took proceedings. However, two entries near the end of his stay perhaps provide an explanation. They state:

August 12th – Went to Reykjavík and instructed Paul Briem in action with B. Sveinson.

August 20th – Law affair with B.S. at (?) –
Briem, Jònsson and Sysselman.

Two days later he packed up and for the first time the total catches are not fully entered in the Register and one wonders why. They did in fact amount to – 506 salmon and grilse – 7208lbs. and 221 trout – 257lbs. There were many more big salmon taken this season including one of 16lb., 3 of 14lb. and several of 13lb and 12lb. There the angling records of James Maitland Burnett end. There were still two more years of his 6-year lease with Olafr to run. There is no evidence of his returning to Iceland and the following account of legal proceedings with which he was involved is probably why.

B.S. was Benedikt Sveinsson and was the owner of Ellidavatn and the waters of Vatnsendi and Árbær. He was a judge of the circuit court in Reykjavík and then became sheriff in northeast Iceland. He was a well-educated man and extremely intelligent. He was the father of the poet Einar Benediktsson who, by many is considered the greatest of all Icelandic poets. But Benedikt Sveinsson was a drinking man, which may have been an explanation for his frequently erratic behaviour. He was well-known for his numerous disputes with many people. Benedikt Sveinsson actually sued Burnett. He claimed that Burnett had let some outsiders fish the Dimá, that he had fished Ellidavatn and Árbær without permission, and that he had spoilt the homefield at Árbær with his tents. Burnett appeared in the court only once (August 20th, 1887), with his interpreter, the Rev. Árni Jónsson, and his lawyer, Mr. Páll Briem, whom he had made his representative on August 12th. Mr. Briem demanded acquittal on all counts, when Sheriff Franz Siemsen finally decided the matter on March 8th, 1888, after seven proceedings before the court plus some production of witnesses before the Reykjavík court. Burnett was acquitted, and Sveinsson had to pay the costs of proceedings. So, although Burnett was acquitted and could therefore have returned to the Dimá, he may have become totally disgusted by the whole matter and also feared further provocation enough so that he didn't care to return.

It is known that Burnett had a predilection for continental life and left London in 1885 to reside on the Continent. There, with the exception of short visits to Scotland, he lived for the rest of his life, mostly in France, Luxemburg, Belgium and Italy. He died in Rome in 1918 at the age of 74.

Chapter 10 – **Icelandic Sea Trout and a Volcanic Eruption**

There's a fisheries conference in Iceland – are you going? Need you ask, when is it? Third week of September. Oh, sugar! The salmon season will be over, but hold on, one will still be able to fish for sea trout, as they enter Iceland's south coast rivers late in the year. A phone call to Arni in Reykjavik confirmed this and, yes, he could fix things. There was a nice little river that entered a lagoon into which the Olfusá-Hvitá flowed. It had a good run of sea trout and the fishing wasn't expensive. He could get tickets and a promise of the loan of waders solved a luggage problem. All I needed to bring was fishing tackle duly disinfected and certified as such by a vet. This met the strict Icelandic law for controlling the possible introduction of fish diseases.

There was once a film entitled "It Always Rains on Sundays". For Iceland delete "on Sundays"! Arni collected me from my comfortable Reykjavik hotel on a dark and very wet morning. Yes, it would clear up, and as we reached the top of the hill going south out of the city his assurances were confirmed. A long stretch of blue sky was starting to emerge in the east from a mass of black cloud. Would it last? The third member of our party was John Waldman, a fisheries biologist from the Hudson River Foundation and angling correspondent for the *New York Times*. Hell, the fish didn't stand a chance.

We were met in Hveragerdi in bright sunshine by Arni's English brother-in-law, Robert, who lived locally, having left London with his Icelandic wife to begin married life in a less stressful environment, sensible fellow. Arni left us under Robert's guidance so he could return to Reykjavik to put the final touches to the conference he was arranging.

The Varma is rather like some of our Scottish west coast rivers. In fact it is almost identical in its features to the Kanaird which flows into Ardmair Bay just north of Ullapool. I knew the Kanaird well when it used to have sea trout, so we could be in for a good day. Because it is a small river and because Icelandic air stewardesses can be most unaccommodating about fishing rods in the aircraft cabin I had brought my seven-piece 8 feet 2 inches Hardy's 'Smuggler' rod packed in my suitcase along with a Sunbeam reel holding a floating line. A box of standard sea trout flies and a Battenkill net completed the outfit. Arni's neoprene waders were going to be a great comfort when the heavens opened.

The river consists of a series of short deep pools and long shallow glides with the pools becoming longer and deeper as one reached its confluence with the lagoon. On reflection a sink-tip line might have been better than a floater but I had to make do. My cast of a teal, blue and silver, black pennell and Connemara black was sufficient unto the day. There was no need for a change of flies. At first, a succession of small trout grabbed the flies and I lost count of numbers released. Then, as the flies swung round from the far bank towards the end of a long glide at the end of a pool, there was an almighty tug and the river's surface erupted as a beautiful silvery fish took to the air where it spent most of its time between short visits to its normal element. Not a big fish, about 1½lb,

Sea trout from the Varma

but a lovely shape. Robert was having similar success in the next pool, but John was still fishless as he persisted in vain with the dry fly, never having fished for sea trout before. It was now time to introduce him to wet flies!

The sky opened and rain reminiscent of a prolonged thundershower whipped the water's surface into foam. A Goretex anorak and Arni's neoprene waders kept me as dry as a bone but poor John was wet to the skin. Nothing ventured nothing gained and I started in at the top of the pool Robert had just vacated. Two-thirds of the way down and mid-way across the pool the line was pulled tight. This was a much bigger fish than the last and was just being brought under control when the weight at the end of the line suddenly increased and bent my poor little 'Smuggler' to a point at which it looked like breaking. There are two fish on! The second was a big brown. How the hell was I going to get two fish into a small Battenkill net? The answer was I wasn't. The sea trout was on the tail fly and the brown on the top dropper. Eventually the 2½lb sea trout slid into the net and the 1¼lb brown trout dangled unceremoniously from the cast as the whole caboodle was rushed ashore.

From the same pool another sea trout of similar weight and two more browns came to the dilapidated teal, blue and silver before the rain stopped. Further downstream John had caught his first-ever sea trout and looked to stay in the river till Domesday. As the sun re-emerged Robert and I broke for coffee during which time he pointed out the towers of steam arising from the geothermal springs about a mile upstream and emphasised how volcanically active this whole area was. I had to make an early return to Reykjavik by the infrequent bus service and Robert went home. We left John on the river "brimming with bright sea trout" as he said later in a *New York Times* article.

On the bus there was a reminder from a neighbouring passenger about volcanic activity. They were expecting something to happen on the south coast. There hadn't been a volcanic eruption for five years and, as these tended to occur every five years, something could happen soon. So it did! Two days later the sub-glacial volcano Grimsvøtn erupted through the Vatnajökull glacier in the south-east of the island. It was the largest eruption in the twentieth century. No salmon rivers are in the vicinity but there is a good sea trout river, the Grenlaekur, just a stone's throw away. Fortunately it wasn't affected by the subsequent severe flooding, but it goes to show that one must be prepared for everything when fishing in Iceland!

Chapter 11 – **Roderick Haig-Brown**

Living in Vancouver as a boy for three years in the early 1930's my introduction to fishing could not have been in a better locality. My only regret has been that more use was not made of this time. Little did I know that an angler and author of the calibre of Roderick Haig-Brown lived and fished so near – Vancouver Island. True, at least I was introduced to a pastime that would influence my future life and career, and what better setting. I still remember a family friend living in the then outbacks of West Vancouver taking me in a canoe to a creek close under the neighbouring mountains to look for young salmon. A party of red indians passed close by and quite unlike those depicted in my story books. Many memories of that time came flooding back on first reading Haig-Brown's *Return to the River* (1942), a saga of a Chinook salmon and almost a Pacific version of Henry Williamson's *Salar the Salmon* (1935). Haig-Brown, too, had written the life story of an Atlantic salmon, entitled *Silver*, four years earlier in 1931. I returned to Vancouver early in 1968 for a salmon conference and visited Vancouver Island where I had a brief try for the early steelheads. Although unsuccessful it gave me a feel for Haig-Brown's fishing and environment where the carcasses of dog salmon were still lying around for scavengers.

Roderick Haig-Brown, like me, was not a Canadian. He was born in England in 1908 and educated at Charterhouse School where his grandfather had been headmaster for some years. His father was a keen angler and wrote *My Game Book* dedicated to his son who, alas, he would never be able to fish with, being killed in 1918. Fortunately, Haig-Brown had two uncles who were keen anglers. They taught him to cast a fly and instilled an enthusiasm for fishing that never left him. His early attempts to catch trout on fly on the Frome closely mirrored mine, and reading these made me remember my own endeavours of trying to cast a dry fly to a rising trout using a 10ft coarse fishing rod and a quite inappropriate weight of line. Blisters were soon in evidence.

As his skill with a dry fly improved during his school holidays so his success in luring trout from the Frome and Itchen became quite impressive and reminded me of my early less successful days on the limestone streams of the Yorkshire dales. Many of these early exploits with a school friend, and the encouragement of kindly landowners, are beautifully told in *A River Never Sleeps* (1946). Early sporting days can always be happier and more memorable if one is fortunate enough to have a mentor, usually elderly, who can give wise guidance and advice and, indeed, secure company, which a parent is not always able to provide. Such a person was Major Greenhill who took over his sporting education. He was already a heroic figure to him for his reputation as one of the best wing shots in England and a fine salmon fisherman. He taught, as good teachers do, by example, by opportune and unhurried explanation, by occasional strong direction.

At the age of 17 Haig-Brown went to the logging-camps of the American Northwest and British Columbia and his angling experiences on the rarely visited streams, rivers and lakes of Vancouver Island fishing for steelheads, cutthroat trout and coho and Tyee salmon are beautifully related in *A River Never Sleeps* and *Fisherman's Summer* (1959). His approach to fishing was the same as mine. He preferred the running water of fast flowing streams and rivers to the stillness of lakes: " A river is water in its loveliest form." However, he was a good lake fisherman and tells of his days and nights camping by many of these remote waters rarely visited by man, an experience I would have enjoyed. Fishing with a dry fly was his favourite method, particularly for cutthroats, but while after steelheads entering the icy rivers in January and February he was not averse to spinning, although even then a heavy fly was preferred. Six-inch spoons were a must for Tyee salmon. He recalls introducing a fishing companion to greased line fishing for summer steelheads. He was not a competitive fisherman and liked to fish by himself or with one or two friends: "Angling is not a competitive sport. The fisherman's only real competition is with his quarry and his only real challenge is the challenge to himself. Nothing can add to this, but the blight of interhuman competition can certainly detract from it."

He also took fishing leisurely: "Dawn can be a beautiful time on the water and I am glad that I have tried early morning fishing as often as I have and in as many different places; but I am glad, too, that I know it is seldom necessary for a fly fisherman to get up early to catch fish, because early rising tends to make work out of pleasure. I like to start comfortably after a good breakfast and that is why I make the broad generalisation that the best fishing hours are likely to come between 10.30am and 4.30pm; certainly a fisherman will be doing his own best work then, and that is at least as important as the mood of the fish." My sentiments entirely.

As a good angler he was aware of and enjoyed his environment and its wildlife and it was so much part of his fishing experience: "I remember the approach to Sandy Pool – under the white-barked alders a floor of freshet-swept sand pierced by bleeding heart and a thousand trilliums and pink Easter lilies just breaking out of bud. Once, going up to the Canyon Pool along the far bank of the river, I crossed a little swamp where skunk cabbage flowers sprang strongly from the black ooze in spaced and loveliest yellow. There is pink almond blossom against blue and white skies. There are killdeer and yellow legs on the tide flats, meadowlarks on the fence posts, red-winged blackbirds in the swamps. Not to go out and meet all this would be a denial of the year's hope."

It was not surprising that he was familiar with the wildlife as, in his early years in British Columbia, he set traplines in the winter and this experience led him to write a number of novels including one for boys – *Starbuck Valley Winter* (1943) which was about cougars and crooks who were robbing the boys' traplines. Canadian wildlife and nomadic people were his subjects for two other books – *Panther* (1934) about a North American mountain lion and *Pool and Rapid* (1932) – the story of a river and its people and wildlife.

I also admire the tremendous powers of observation he possessed, both in seeing rising fish and detecting their presence on the river bed or lake bottom and their slightest movement to his fly, and also noticing other creatures going about their business whether they were bears, coons, cougars or mink. He was a compassionate angler and exercised restraint in the size of his catch both in quantity and quality.

He wrote 24 books during his busy life and probably his magnum opus was *The Western Angler: An account of Pacific Salmon and Western Trout* (1939). *Life* magazine referred to him as the most eloquent of modern-day fishing prose writers. Besides having been in the Canadian army, and seconded to the Royal Canadian Mounted Police, he also served as a magistrate and judge, and was Chancellor of the University of Victoria. He was also on the International

Pacific Salmon Fisheries Commission and it would have been interesting to have had his views on fishing matters as a commissioner during a leisurely lunch-break from fishing his favourite Campbell River beside which he lived for many years.

His last book *Bright Waters, Bright Fish* was completed just one month before he died suddenly in 1976. It was published in 1980 and is a most significant work. It is said to be "the testament of a man who passionately believed that it is the responsibility of all citizens, from fishermen and politicians, to protect and perpetuate the sport fishing resource;.....its values, traditions, standards and ethics – belong to the anglers themselves and is in the care and keeping of anglers everywhere."

Chapter 12 – Amid the High Hills

We parked the Landrover at the stalker's house at Inverchorain and set off with our fishing gear up Glenchorain. After crossing the stream it was a gentle walk along the glen with steep sloping hills on either side. Some stags were sitting on the tops to the left of us but were too far away to show any concern at our presence. At the head of the glen it was a steep climb. Reaching the top we stopped to catch our breath and look back at the view which was quite spectacular. Over the brow of the hill one could look down on Glen Orrin and Loch na Caoidhe which was sparkling in the summer sun. I was to fish this loch and the little Loch am Fiar, a short distance downstream, with Brodde, a Swedish student, two years later. Our catch on that day was over 50 trout. Orme Armstrong and I fished it one day four years later and took 60 trout. However, our destination today was An Gorm Loch high up among the hills on the far side of Glen Orrin. It was a steep descent to the loch and then a walk along the loch side and on by the River Orrin. After crossing the river a short distance downstream of the loch we headed for the burn flowing out of An Gorm and climbed steeply up to more level ground and followed the stream to the loch. Small trout darted for cover as we walked along the streamside. It was obviously a good spawning burn. A short climb to the brow of the hill and there was the loch looking very much like a jewel as it is called in the gaelic.

Robert put the cans of lager in the loch to cool and, after a cup of tea, we tackled up. I was using a trusty 8½ft. split cane rod given me by Phil Lupton a tackle dealer in Harrogate as recompense for my beloved 8½ft. greenheart smashed in transit by British Rail. The trout would be pretty uneducated and traditional loch flies were selected. A Blue Zulu as a bob fly, however, was a must. The loch is almost circular so there were no definite headlands from which to fish or any weedy bays to try. However, as it turned out fish seemed to be in all parts of the loch with perhaps a preference for the shallow area at the top near a small inflowing stream. The attributes of these small hill lochs are their remoteness and tranquility. In the case of the loch we were fishing there was no road between Strathconon to the north and Strathfarrar to the south. The few habitations, such as Cabaan, in the glen are now deserted. An old man in Strathconon remembers the time when, if there was a funeral in the glen, the coffin with its bearers had to cross the river on stilts. Further downstream is the Orrin Dam built by the North of Scotland Hydro-electric Board. One Saturday afternoon one of the consulting engineers to this scheme and I walked through Glenchorain and down Glen Orrin to the dam. The most memorable part of the walk was passing in the evening through a herd of red deer hinds with their fawns who were quite unperturbed by our presence.

By lunchtime half a dozen 8 to 10 oz. trout were on the bank, nearly all taken on the Blue Zulu. After a very relaxed lunch and absorbing all the lager fishing recommenced and in another couple of hours we had a further five fish of about the same weight range. We had been told there were large fish in the loch as indeed there may have been at one time. However, with the amount of spawning available in the stream recruitment to the loch would have been very good. Therefore, without adequate exploitation and a good food supply, there would be insufficient food to go round for the increased population and hence lower growth rates, with few fish reaching a very large size. As on so many

The magic hour approaches. The artist has captured in this watercolour the atmosphere of an early summer evening on a hill loch close to the time when one can expect the trout to start rising.

estates during the war very few folk, if any, fished these waters and so the trout populations increased and their average weight declined. It used to be a practice of estate workers to transport some of the fish from overstocked lochs to those where there were no available spawning sites and hence very few fish. The introduced fish had little competition from the small native stock, assuming there was one, and so there was adequate food for good growth. Finding one of these lochs previously stocked in this way was something of a reward as frequently good-sized trout were caught. Lochs where there was a remarkable increase in trout growth rate were those which had had their levels raised by impoundment with dam construction for hydro power. In such cases trout swam out over the newly flooded ground and hoovered up the earthworms and crane fly larvae, which came out of the flooded pasture. Their growth rates were initially phenomenal but sadly as this terrestrial food source diminished growth rates could not be maintained. In other parts of the Highlands there are many lochs where the average weight of trout is very good, particularly in the limestone lochs of Durness in Sutherland. The weights of trout to be expected in Scottish trout lochs can be found in Bruce Sandison's excellent book *The Trout Lochs of Scotland*. As there was a long walk ahead of us, we packed up and retraced our steps but, after crossing the Orrin, took a slightly longer but less steep path back to Inverchorain.

Working for some years in mid-Ross it was a delight after an evening meal to drive up Strathconon with a colleague and explore some of the small hill lochs that had become accessible as a result of construction work during hydro power scheme development. Trout were abundant in most of them and, while not large, provided good sport and a welcome supplement to one's diet in the days before the advent of supermarkets. There were always surprises and on one, a Loch uillt ghuibhais, I caught two trout, each weighing a pound. The colouring of one was most unusual, being dark bronze with only a very few small black spots on its sides. The capture of such an unusually coloured trout, whatever its weight, was a reward in itself.

Loch a' Mhuillin was a favourite spot for evening fishing. I first got to know of it from Capt. Ron Morrison, a veteran of the Royal Flying Corps. He lived in a white croft, a short distance below Meig Dam and beside the Strathconon road. RWG, as he was called, was one of the trapwatchers on the nearby experimental fish trap operating on the Meig at that time. He was a most interesting man but could talk the hindleg off a donkey. He kept goats and supplied us with fresh goats' milk. Access to the loch was rather like an assault course. It started by crossing the fields to Morrison's croft, avoiding the Billy goat as one went. Then, after cutting short a prolonged conversation with Morrison, scaling a 10-ft. deer fence. After this, there was a steep climb through the heather and aiming for a narrow cleft between two hills. The loch was the other side of the hills and was quite sheltered by the surrounding terrain. It was a favourite loch to which to take visitors keen to catch a trout. Usually there was little sign of activity until day was drawing to a close. Then, as though one had turned on a switch, fish would start rising and the rings of rising fish would cover the whole loch surface. The fish were not particular about fly pattern and one usually caught fish. The best catch Orme and I had one evening was 28 trout between 8 and 12 oz.

There were so many things to see while fishing these remote waters. Plant life, while not luxuriant, was most interesting. There were a number of aquatic species such as bog lobelia and insectivorous ones like the deep red sundew with small sticky tentacles for catching unwary flies and the milkwort with its pale green rosette of leaves shaped like a starfish and its upright purple flower. On the high and more barren ground one could find the glossy black fruit of the crowberry. There was also always the chance of coming across a sprig of white heather. Some lochs are very popular with waterfowl, particularly in the Shetlands and Outer Isles and many is the time I've been privileged to have the company of red and black-throated divers. The attention of the great skua or bonxie is less welcome and can make fishing certain parts of a loch most unpleasant. Black-headed gulls and common terns are rather like noisy children and have to be tolerated and one certainly doesn't feel lonely when they're on the loch. Then there are the deer, occasionally a jolly otter and, if lucky, a crafty fox. They say that if you feel you're being watched and yet can see no one, then it is assuredly a fox whose doing the watching. Two useful items to take with one on the hill are an Ordnance Survey map and a compass. They are useful to navigate from one loch to another and, indeed, to find a loch not previously visited. If a mist comes down while miles from home then the compass may become a lifesaver. They say that to fish these remote areas is to consummate one's angling life. I heartily agree.

Chapter 13 – **The Night Dwellers**

In my early years as an angler and living in the centre of England sea trout seemed far beyond one's reach. They were spoken of in awe and dreams of night fishing for these wonderful creatures were frequent. One read of them in books such as B.B.'s *The Fisherman's Bedside Book* and looked at them eagerly when they appeared on the fishmonger's slab, which they did from time to time during the war. While serving in the R.A.F. I met up with an Australian pilot and keen angler who had spent some time at R.A.F. Kinloss in Morayshire, not far from the Findhorn. The conversation came round to sea trout. Yes, they were there for the taking at the mouth of that river. They were mostly finnock, although larger ones were caught during spates in the Brodie Burn. Tickets were available at the tackle shop in Forres, which was a nice town in which to stay. Forres was a long way from my base at R.A.F. Lindholme near Doncaster. How was one to get there? Apparently travel warrants issued when going on leave were made out to the destination at which you intended residing while on leave. Why then didn't I make out my leave residence as Forres? No problem, and late summer saw me travelling overnight to Edinburgh and on north through the wilds of Scotland of which one had always dreamt. After changing somewhere along the line, it may have been Aviemore; Forres was finally reached.

One thing was soon to be made clear to me and would be a warning for future outings after sea trout – the tide. Going down to the estuary the first evening my attention was riveted on the numerous finnock jumping and the thrill when they grabbed hold of the red and silver terrors which had been recommended. A few fish were in my bag and time passed so quickly that it was almost dark before I realised that the river seemed to be getting deeper. The pool had a small island which lay between me and the shore, that island now seemed smaller, the tide was coming in! By the grace of God a torch shone higher up the river and after a desperate call the torch started to come towards me. It was a local angler who must have realised that some silly visitor was trying to drown himself. By his shining the torch down on the water I was able to find a way across to the bank by the shallowest route but not before shipping gallons of water into my waders. The remainder of the week was spent behaving more sensibly and still enjoying sport with the delightful finnock, which the hotel cooked for all the guests for breakfast.

It was some years later before there was a renewed introduction to sea trout. This time it was on the Conon estuary. The Bridge Pool at Conon Bridge and the subsequent pools right down to the estuary provide good sea trout fishing. A Findhorn episode occurred yet again. Fishing below the Bridge Pool in a rather narrow long pool restricted on the right bank by a tree-clad island the river level started to rise. As high tide was still some way off it eventually dawned on me that this rise was due to power generation at Tor Achilty Power Station some miles upstream. Although a hooter warns anglers just below the power station that generation is about to start, there is unfortunately no means of notifying anglers further downstream. The only safe measure is to phone the power station before fishing to find out if and when generation is likely to begin. Having lunch with me and, as the fishing was good, the island made a good safe haven and one could wait until generation ceased which wasn't too long.

The opportunity to fish for sea trout from a boat seemed a good idea after the previous experiences. Ken Balmain, a colleague working with me in the north, knew the head ghillie at Scourie in charge of the fishing at Loch Stack in Sutherland. It was arranged that we drive over there for a night's fishing. We would go out in a boat after the day fishers had come in. Our mode of conveyance was Duncan McIver's new Morris Minor which, because it was still running in, he would not drive at more than 40 mph. There is a saying: "there's no speed north of Dunkeld", how right it is. It is a goodish run from Strathpeffer to Scourie but we eventually made it and enjoyed a most welcome tea at the Scobie's house by the side of the loch. There was no hurry to get on the water, as there would be little activity until it was dark. Ken had tied up some hefty flies that were a cross between a bumble and a Loch Ordie and these were put on. We were all using rods of 10½ or 11ft, mine was a new Hardy's Viscount Grey. Shortly after dark fish started to show and it was not long before Duncan had a good 3lb. sea trout. Soon we were all in business and it required a certain amount of discipline in casting to avoid hooking each other's lines which would have led to a waste of fishing time and short tempers. Most of the time one of us would be playing a fish which, in the dark required co-operation from the others to help in netting in the dark. Time went all too quickly and because of the new Morris Minor's requirements we headed south just before dawn. It had been a grand night and there were some splendid sea trout to show for our joint efforts.

The next boat experience was on Loch Doule situated on the River Carron in Wester Ross. Unfortunately it was a very bright August day and there was little breeze. It was a surprise then when, before even the ghillie had rowed far from the shore, a sea trout of 4lb. 10oz. took my Black Pennell. This was a good start with promises of a good day that didn't, however, materialise. Two more fish of 1½lb. were taken and a number of finnock. It was a lot of hard work with the ghillie keeping me at it and, as a Viscount Grey is not a light rod, signs of "tennis elbow" started to develop. A few days later I ordered a handle to screw into the butt of the rod from Hardy's to make it double-handed. This was a great improvement and turned it into a good little salmon rod.

Another loch on the Carron and lying further upstream is Loch Scaven. This was not as good a sea trout loch as Doule but did yield some good fish and fished best on a rough day. One evening Jimmy Younger senior and I fished it and were frustrated by getting huge rises to our flies. It was almost as though someone had thrown a brick in above the fly. When one struck there was no connection with a fish. After a great deal of trying I did manage to catch one of 3½lb. on a Blue Zulu. We were told later that when a fish rose you should recite the first verse of the National Anthem before striking. That requires a great deal of will power!

Although sea trout fishing from a boat is most pleasant and can be very productive, weather can sometimes force one ashore and then it is a matter of resorting to bank fishing, as happened to me in Connemara while fishing loughs Invermore and Lurgeen, as well as on Loch Scaven. It is then one wishes one was fishing a river. Certainly I've had my best days river fishing. The little River Kanaird north of Ullapool provided some pleasant times with sea trout, with fish up to nearly 4lb. frequently being caught. Fishing the lower Kanaird was like being in a time warp and the rasping call of the corncrake was a welcome sound. It was easy to cover the pools and a joy to fish at night when you often shared the river with a family of otters. One night I disturbed an otter with a fish down in the estuary. He left the fish on the bank to retreat out to a bed of seaweed and there, with only his head showing, spat at me, probably annoyed at the thought of losing his fish. Sometimes they would be in the pool you were fishing and on one occasion one got hooked to my cast but, after wondering how one landed an otter, it fortunately broke the barb of the teal, blue and silver and disappeared. On another occasion my wife and I were having our lunch by the river when an otter swam into the pool and was quite unaware of our presence as it worked upstream. One could continue to catch fish even though an otter had been present. In those days, before there were salmon farms in Ardmair Bay, sea trout could be caught spinning from the shore.

My first introduction to the Border Esk was through Oliver Williams who rented the Irvine House beat. I could take a friend and spend the day and, more importantly, the night, fishing. Chris and I drove down from Edinburgh and arrived in the late morning. It was a very bright and hot day and most of the daylight hours, after an inspection of the river, were spent relaxing in folding chairs brought with us together with a table and primus. We'd seen shoals of sea trout lying close in by the willows in one pool and seen one or two salmon jump. Two aldermanic chub were watched herding a shoal of minnows for their coming meal and one of us caught a dace. So there was no shortage of fish life. The only humans enjoying the water were a group of bathers, which made fishing the pool they were wallowing in out of the question until dark. However, we would wait – until darkness descended. It is a great temptation to start to fish just too soon at night and one has to be firm and wait until it is really dark. The ghost moths were floating up and down in a nearby field with its resident donkey just visible in the gloaming. We wandered down to the river. We had put up casts of three flies of mallard and claret, dark mackerel and teal, blue and silver. It's not always wise to have three flies on the cast as it is more likely to tangle and time consuming to unravel. When this does happen it's better to discard the cast, putting it in a box for dealing with back home, and tie on a new one. Two flies on a cast are less likely to cause trouble. I did untangle a friend's cast once with a great deal of patience. When I got in a fankle no amount of patience would sort it and the torchlight threw so many shadows it was difficult to tell which was cast and which was shadow. Chris waded in to fish across to the willows while I went further downstream to fish a slightly deeper pool with a rather difficult bank which would cause problems when it came to landing fish. We agreed that whenever one of us caught four fish they should let the other one know and, if agreeable, change ends as it were. It was a beautiful night with the suggestion of mist coming off the water, which we're told is a bad sign for good fishing. It was not the case this time and soon a fresh 2lb. sea trout was on the bank. It was difficult to land, as it was deepish water in by the bank that was rather steep at that point. Some folk carry a torch to help them see the fish, but I find a bicycle lamp hanging around one's neck by a piece of cord leaves both hands free. After catching three more fish, which were landed without trouble, I joined Chris who had taken half a dozen and showed no sign of moving. I left him to it and returned downstream where two more fish of about 2lb. were landed. Dawn was fast approaching and the mist was getting thicker so it was time to go back to the car and get the primus going for a cup of tea before the drive home. Chris appeared with seven fish and was as happy as Larry. The seventy or so miles drive home after being on the river the best part of twenty hours inevitably means that there is a good chance of dozing off. It was my usual practice after driving a score or so miles to pull in and have forty winks. This was sufficient to charge my batteries and see me home without driving off the road.

My day's fishings given me by Oliver in the next few summers followed much the same pattern. Sometimes the weather was cloudy and the river low. It was then possible to catch sea trout on dry fly during the day, although night-time gave the best results. The occasional brown trout was often caught and ended up in the frying pan over the primus for the evening meal before the night's fishing. When the sky was overcast, nights were so dark that it was like casting blind into a void. One had only a slight inkling as to the distance you were casting and the general direction of the line. The first indication that your line was in the water and fishing was a few slight plucks. They might be slight but they merited a strike, upon which there was usually quite a commotion the other end and you were literally playing a fish blind. Gradually the resistance lessened and the splash of the fish as it came to the bank signalled it was time to switch on the lamp hanging round one's neck and net the fish. It was usual to fish a floating line, although on one occasion when Bill Currie and I were fishing Bill used a sinking line. Between us we had 17 fish, I had nine and Bill eight. However, Bill's were slightly larger and we put this down to the fact that his line was fishing deeper and picking up the bigger fish. A word of warning, the one disadvantage of fishing deep, as Bill found out to his cost, is that there is the risk of catching a nocturnal eel. Eels, besides putting up a dogged fight, get your cast into one hell of a mess.

There was one occasion on the Border Esk when fishing during the day was very good. This was because the river flow was moderating after a flood and the sea trout were on the move, as quite a few were caught in the fast water between pools where fish are not normally taken.

Inevitably one associates sea trout with dark nights. There is no more agreeable way to fish for them than at such times. However, my largest sea trout was caught at noon on a bright summer's day. I was fishing for salmon on Upper Pavilion on Tweed a short distance above the Melrose Bridge and had on a Garry Dog dressed on a size 10 treble hook. Towards the bottom of the Quarry Pool my line was pulled out by something with the speed of an express train and didn't stop until it was well below the pool and heading for Meg's. It was now a matter of getting the fish back upstream. Fortunately it obliged by racing upstream in the direction of Galashiels. This rushing about soon tired the fish and it was drawn slowly towards the shelving gravel. All the time it was churning the water into a sea of foam. It was eventually beached and turned the scales at 12lb. Its scales were read by Ronald Campbell of the Tweed Foundation. It was found to be a little over six years old, having spent three years in the river as a parr and three plus years at sea. It had not spawned previously. Laphroaig generously 'did the honours', courtesy of *Trout and Salmon*.

Chapter 14 – **Rod, Book and Net**

Back in 1978 and 1979 as a group of keen John Buchan enthusiasts we used to meet up in one or other of our houses to discuss arrangements for setting-up a John Buchan Society. The leader of our discussions and originator of the idea of such a society was Dr. Eileen Stewart, who was reading for a Ph.D. at Edinburgh University on an aspect of Buchan's work. She was also an English teacher at George Watson's College. The group consisted of the author, Trevor Royle, a financial expert, a member of the Robert Louis Stevenson Club and myself, an avid collector of Buchan's works and a keen angler.

It was in the latter capacity that I came into my own in Society business. This connection arose during the planning of the John Buchan Day that was to be the inauguration of the John Buchan Society. The day was to consist of talks and also a display of memorabilia relating to the author. I knew Toby Buchan, son of William Buchan and a nephew of the second Lord Tweedsmuir, through his seeing one of my books through the publisher Cassell for whom he worked. Toby was able to produce some excellent photos of John Buchan and the family fishing and also John Buchan's fishing rod!

The John Buchan Day held on 3rd March, 1979, was a great success. The Rt. Hon. Lord Tweedsmuir, son of John Buchan, kindly presided over the proceedings, in the course of which the constitution was circulated and a committee elected.

Because John Buchan was a keen angler and almost always included angling episodes in his novels, I decided that we must have an annual angling event at which like-minded members could get together and fish in friendly competition and end the day over a meal in pleasant surroundings. It was hoped that there were enough members who engaged in the gentle art. It would also be good if we had a trophy for which we could compete. A whisky company in Glasgow gave monthly prizes of their product to anglers catching the largest salmon, sea trout and brown/rainbow trout each month. Having received such a prize, I knew who to contact and a friendly conversation with Hector MacLennan, sales manager of Ballantine's Whisky, resulted in the promise of a trophy in the form of a Quaich to be known as the Ballantine's Whisky Angling Trophy. This was duly presented to the Society at one of its business meetings and received on behalf of the Society by Lady Susan Douglas-Hamilton, wife of the Rt. Hon. Lord James Douglas-Hamilton one of our Council members.

The day for our first angling outing arrived. The venue was Talla Reservoir at the head of Tweed and not far from Tweedsmuir. It is a long stretch of water with a rocky shoreline with a good head of trout although the fish were not of a very large size. It was a dull sort of day and our bevy of anglers plied their art industriously but for little reward and six anglers could only produce two trout for their efforts. The winner was a Mr. George Grenfell with one trout slightly heavier than the fish caught by the runner-up. The second prize was a copy of *John MacNab*, very appropriate. Mr. Ross, chief executive of the Scottish Tourist Board, made the trophy presentation, after which we all retired to the *Crook Inn* for a convivial Scottish high tea where we were joined by non-fishing members of the Society.

The venue for the 1981 get-together, North Esk Reservoir near Penicuik, was a non-event with only four anglers and no fish. However, in September, with more members we took to the water at Glencorse Reservoir nestled among the Pentland Hills. This is a deep water with very little shallow area except at the top end where a small stream enters. On this occasion more fish were caught and I was the winner of the trophy and Richard, the runner-up, received a copy of Buchan's *Montrose*. To end the day, a pleasant meal was had at *Habbie's Howe*, a neighbouring hostelry.

Significant weights of brown trout were caught at our 1982 event held at Gladhouse Reservoir situated in the Moorfoot Hills. This is the best of the Edinburgh reservoirs for trout fishing. It is a fairly shallow reservoir with plenty of feeding for the trout. There is a good inflowing stream providing good spawning ground for the fish. It is a popular place for geese in the winter. We hoped for spectacular results as we had a new member by the name of Richard Hannay fishing with us! However, a Gerald Barry caught the most browns using fairly large patterns of Grouse and Claret, Heckham and Green and Greenwell. The post-fishing celebrations were again held at *Habbie's Howe*.

The 1983 gathering was held in May and Gladhouse was once more the venue. It was an extremely wet day and, arriving late, I found that the other members had taken to the water and left me the heaviest boat to row on my own. Having rowed in university college eights on the Thames this should have been no problem. However, this boat was built more like a whaler and was a heavy old cow. The massive oars were designed so that one man used each oar and not one man to two oars. The only consolation was that she could take on a lot of water before I need think of bailing and in today's condition this was going to be an advantage. The water was almost flat calm and the rings of rising trout were hardly distinguishable from the rings made by the heavy rain. A cast made up of a Blae and Black, Heckham and Red and Dark Mackerel was put up, as the fish here seemed to go for traditional loch flies. My first three fish, all of ½lb., came to the Blae and Black. The fish were rising to some small flies on the surface, so the Dark Mackerel was taken off and a Sand Fly was put on the top dropper. The change had an immediate effect and a fish of 15oz. was soon netted, followed by another of 14oz. My "barge" was drifting towards the large island so some effort was made to row back towards the main centre of fish activity. Once back a trout of 1lb 2oz. joined the others. As six fish were now lying in the boat, I called across to a boat just within hailing distance and asked if there was a bag limit for the water. The question was met with a peal of laughter. No chance of getting your limit today in this weather, no way! The rain was not lessening and the Barbour jacket, deerstalker and waterproof trousers were beginning to let in the water in a very generous manner. Over the next couple of water-sodden hours four more fish came aboard and then it was decided to call it a day by a combination of semaphore and shouting. A very sodden group of Buchanites retired to the fishing hut where a good meal had been prepared. Our total catch was 17 of which I had taken 10 that made me the trophy winner.

Since then these angling events have been held irregularly and with varying success. Lord Tweedsmuir, a keen angler, joined one such outing at Megget Reservoir near St. Mary's Loch in the Scottish Borders. Alas, the wind rose to gale force and the day had to be abandoned. The John Buchan Society has now a worldwide membership of over 470 so there is no reason why this angling get-together should not be held in other parts of the United Kingdom, or even abroad – Canada would be a good venue!

Chapter 15 – **John Buchan and the Flyfishers' Club**

The Flyfishers' Club, a London-based institution, was founded in 1884 "to bring together gentlemen devoted to flyfishing generally and to afford a ready means of communication between those interested in the delightful art…" The Annual Dinner of the Club has been held every year since 1885, with the exception of the war years. Since 1932, its venue has been the Savoy Hotel, where a large company comes to honour, as their principal guest, some distinguished speaker – who is, most often, a fisherman. Among those who have presided, or been guests of honour, have been HRH Duke of York (later King George VI), the Rt. Hon. Stanley Baldwin, Viscount Grey, Lord MacMillan, Lord Home and – John Buchan.

The 1932 summer issue of *The Journal of the Flyfishers' Club* reports that: "The Annual Dinner of the Club was held this year at the Savoy Hotel on February 25th. Mr. John Buchan was the guest of the evening and over a hundred and eighty of us mustered at the tables to do him honour." The account that follows is reproduced from that Journal, and as a member of the Flyfishers' Club I should like to thank our past secretary, Commander Norman Fuller, for his search of the archives.

After the PRESIDENT of the Club, Brigadier-General Banon, had given the loyal toast, the CHAIRMAN, the Hon. Mr. Justice Farwell, proposed the toast of "Our guests" and, in concluding, remarked "But whether our guests are Flyfishers or not I am sure that they are the most estimable of fellows and, therefore, I ask the members of the Club to charge their glasses and drink with the utmost goodwill to the toast of "Our guests", coupled with the name of Mr. John Buchan. (Applause). The toast was drunk with cordiality.

Mr. BUCHAN, on rising to reply, was received with loud applause. He said –

'Mr. Chairman and Gentlemen, - It is my pleasant duty on behalf of the guests to thank the Club for the hospitality they have extended to us tonight, and to thank Mr. Justice Farwell for his good wishes. We are all deeply conscious of the honour of having our health proposed by a Judge of the High Court. I hope that he will soon be a Lord Justice like his distinguished father. (Hear, hear). A judge is usually supposed to be remarkable for sobriety - we talk of being as sober as a judge, while a lord is believed to be exactly the opposite – we talk of being as drunk as a lord (Laughter). A Lord Justice would therefore seem to strike the happy mean – that genial sobriety, that reasoned hilarity, which Mr. Justice Farwell has exhibited in his speech tonight. (Hear, hear and laughter)

"I am greatly honoured to be your guest tonight, but I am also abashed, for, though I have fished with a fly since I was nine years of age, I can lay no claim either to the expert knowledge or the technical skill of many of those whom I see around me. But, Gentlemen, I take it that the passport to your friendship is not supreme skill or supreme knowledge, but the proper attitude of mind. To that, I believe, I have some claim. I would rather be by the waterside than anywhere in the world. (Applause) I remember Lord Grey of Falloden telling me once that during a hot August which he had to spend in the House of Commons he found a remote corner where he could hear a dripping tap and there he used to ensconce himself and shut his eyes and imagine that he was beside a Northumberland burn. That is the proper spirit. (Hear, hear) There was a famous Tweedside angler many years ago called Thomas Stoddart, who wrote some excellent fishing verse. A friend of his youth met him one day and asked what was his profession. "Profession!" he exclaimed in astonishment, "Man, I am an angler." I say ditto to Mr. Stoddart. (Applause)

"I like to catch fish by any legitimate method. (Laughter) I have even dabbled in illegitimate methods, for at the age of sixteen on Tweedside I was arrested for poaching salmon by burning the water. (Loud laughter). The result was that when I stood for Parliament for that county just before the war, I had the poaching vote to a man. (Renewed laughter)

"What are the reasons why angling is such a profound passion with people like ourselves, why, more than any other sport, it has been consecrated by great literature? There are several causes. It takes us at all hours and at all seasons into the secret recesses of nature. It provides us with a chance of peace without boredom, leisure for reflection combined with a perpetual gentle excitement. It is a sport which we can pursue to the end of our days. You cannot play Rugby football much after thirty, or attempt serious courses of mountaineering much after fifty, or stalk the high tops when your wind is short and the flesh is burdensome. But you can fish as long as your legs can support you and your arm is strong enough to cast a fly. (Applause)

"I would add another cause. Angling provides us with an intellectual exercise, the most difficult study in the world, far more intricate than Einstein's mathematics or Professor Eddington's physics – the psychology of fish.

"I have sometimes reflected on the relationship between angling and morals. It is clearly a real one, but how are we to explain it? Izaak Walton often refers to a friend as "a good man and an angler". He might have left out the first epithet, for it is to be presumed, if his friend was an angler, he would certainly be a good man. Did anyone ever know of a bad angler in literature or life? I never have. I have known good shots who were indifferent characters and golfers who were great rascals, but I have never known or heard of a wicked angler. (Laughter)

"You remember a passage in Scott's *St. Ronan's Well*, which I have always regarded as one of the classic laudations of our craft. It is Meg Dods who is speaking, the mistress of the Cleikum Inn, and she is describing the fraternity of anglers who used to come there to fish the Tweed:

> *"They were pawky auld carles, that kend whilk side their bread was buttered upon. They were up in the morning – had their parritch, wi maybe a thimbleful of brandy and then awa' up into the hills, eat their bit of cauld meat on the heather, and came hame at e'en wi the creel full of caller trouts, and had them to their dinner, and their quiet cogue of ale and their drap punch and were set singing their catches and glee, as they ca'd them, till ten o'clock, and then to bed, wi God bless ye – and what for no?"*

"What for no?" indeed! That is a description of that happy life. That is the ideal cherished by every honest man, and I am sure that it is the ideal of this Club which has so generously entertained us."

The PRESIDENT then rose and gave the toast of "The Flyfishers' Club". In his concluding remarks, and turning to John Buchan, he said: "We have been fortunate in our guests, and we hope they have enjoyed their dinner as much as we have their company. (Hear, hear). We are grateful to Mr. Buchan for representing the guests tonight in such an excellent speech. (Applause). We have read his books with delight. Sometimes it is not advisable to meet a favourite author in the flesh, but after tonight we shall read John Buchan's books with even greater pleasure. (Applause). As a small token of appreciation, and in accordance with the custom of the Club, I have to present our guest with a fly as a memento of this dinner."

General Banon handed the fly to Mr. Buchan amid great applause.

The CHAIRMAN, proceeding, said: "The occasion has been too much for our Club poet, Dr. Barton, who has struck his lyre and burst into song. He – I should say it – is a pleasing lyre. (Laughter). And this is what he sings:

> *Not for itself, but in appreciation*
> *Of all we owe to your delightful pen,*
> *Accept this token of initiation*
> *Into the brotherhood of fishermen.*
> *Whether you conjure up our tears of laughter*
> *Whether we turn the page with smile or sigh,*
> *In earnest of our kindly thought hereafter,*
> *We give, as emblem of our Craft, this fly.*   (Applause)

"The fly is tied by Sir Francis Colchester Wemyss, who, we regret, cannot be present tonight owing to illness. He has called it the "Buchaneer" (Laughter). Curiously enough he spelt it with a 'ch' instead of the usual 'cc'. This is, I suppose, a subtle allusion to the Companionship of Honour bestowed by His Majesty on our guest two days ago. (Applause). We hope the 'Buchaneer' may make many captures. (Applause). Lest you, Sir, have not a pocket large enough to carry away this souvenir I have here another emblem of our craft, a fishing bag, presented by a member of this Club who wishes to remain anonymous. I hope that you may live many years to fill this at the river-side." (Applause).

Footnote: John Buchan's eldest son, the Rt. Hon. The Lord Tweedsmuir, became a member of the Flyfishers' Club in 1948 and was its President in 1960.

Chapter 16 – **Angling on the 39 Steps**

John Buchan's role as guest speaker at the Flyfishers' Club dinner at the Savoy in 1932 was well-deserved recognition of his prowess as an angler as much of that as his status as a writer. The frequency of references to angling in his many novels is not generally realised. The salmon 'poaching' foray in *John MacNab* (1925) will have been read with amusement by four or five generations of anglers, and his early angling anthology *Musa Piscatrix* (1896) has given lasting pleasure to many. His *Scholar Gipsies*, published in the same year, recalls some angling incidents on his beloved Tweed. Some will have read his erudite introduction to the Oxford University Press edition of *The Compleat Angler* (1935) and noted, no doubt, his comment:

> " To men with gypsy blood, life must be a dull business if it is confined to urban streets and the routine of affairs; yet to a man given brain and will, there is the work before him which he cannot shirk. Hence comes the angler – the sportsman, I love to think, who can feel all the primeval excitement of his sport, and yet the man of culture to whom nature is more than a chalk stream or salmon river, who has ears for Coridon's song as well as the plash of trout below the willows."

Those who have read this introduction and also the chapter on fishing, particularly the section entitled *Lost Monsters* in his *Great Hours of Sport* (1921) I am sure are saddened that he never completed his planned angling book *Pilgrim's Rest*, the two completed chapters of which appear at the end of *Memory Hold the Door* (1940).

However, let us explore his novels and meet those characters that liked to wield a rod. There are many. One of J.B's first novels, *John Burnet of Barns* (1898) was set in upper Tweeddale and he is probably recalling some of his early exploits as a youth when staying with his grandparents near Dawyck when he describes in the first chapter young John Burnet's capture of a large Tweed trout:

> "I prepared my tackle on the grass, making a casting line of fine horse hair which I had plucked from our own grey gelding. I had no such fine hooks as folk nowadays bring from Edinburgh, sharpened and barbed ready to their hand; but rough home-made ones which Tam Todd, the land grieve, had fashioned out of old needles. My line was of thin stout whipcord, to which I had made the casting firm with a knot of my own invention. I had out my bag of worms and, choosing a fine red one, made it fast on the hook…I had not sat many minutes before the rod was wrenched violently downwards, nearly swinging me from my perch. I have got a monstrous trout, I thought…. He ran up the water and down; then far below the tree roots, from whence I had much difficulty in forcing him; then he thought to break my line by rapid jerks, but he did not know the strength of my horse hair. By and by he grew wearied, and I landed him comfortably on a spit of land – great red-spotted fellow with a black back."

Such youthful accounts, reminiscent of J.B.'s early days, occur frequently in his later books when he becomes a father with three sons. He dedicates *The Island of Sheep* (1936) to J.N.S.B., his eldest son Johnnie, the second Lord Tweedsmuir and a distinguished past president of the Flyfishers' Club. It is probably Johnnie who is portrayed as Peter John in *The Island of Sheep*, and who is the son of Richard Hannay, the hero of the *Thirty-nine Steps* (1915). Hannay says of his son:

> "Peter John's lack of scholastic success used to worry Mary sometimes, but I felt he was going his own way and picking up a pretty good education. He was truthful and plucky and kindly …. He scarcely knew a bat from a ball, but he could cast a perfect dry fly."

Later in the book the Hannay family and friends have to take sanctuary in Scotland (in Tweeddale where else?) and Hannay remarks that "the streams were low and the fishing poor, though Peter John did fairly well in the lochs and got a three pounder one evening in the park lake with a dry fly."

Although Peter John first appears in *The Three Hostages* (1924) it is another youngster, Davie, one of the hostages, keen on fishing and natural history, who has the greater share of attention. He, too, did not have a distinguished school career but "he was a great fisherman and had killed a lot of trout with the fly on hill burns in Galloway". Hannay remarks: "And as the father spoke I suddenly began to realise the little chap and to think he was just the kind of boy I wanted Peter John to be."

General Hannay was not a keen angler himself, although he took a great interest in the sport and even participated in fishery management. In the *Three Hostages"* he spent "a supremely muddy and wet afternoon putting Loch Leven fry into a pond." He obviously had a great respect for anglers. In *Mr. Standfast* (1919) he says of an eccentric character, who he found rather a bore: "When we went back to the hall he announced that he must get on the road…..it appeared he was staying at an inn a dozen miles off for a couple of days' fishing, and the news somehow made me like him better."

The exploits of another angler are described vividly in *The Long Traverse* (1941). It is set in Canada and young Donald, the central character like Peter John, was not an academic success. It is strange that none of Buchan's young anglers were academically inclined, but perhaps this is not significant! However, Donald was an enthusiastic angler, which is apparent from Chapter 1, although:

> "He has never yet caught a salmon, and the salmon rods were in his father's case, but he could try for a monster with his own little greenheart….There was a swirl at the tail of the pool above the rapids and his heart jumped, for he saw that it was a big fish. An unpleasing recollection followed on the thrill. The sight of the moving salmon reminded him of an interview which had preceded his departure. His last term's school report had been shocking."

This has a familiar ring about it! An interesting episode occurs in *The Long Traverse* when Donald is taken to the Grand Lac de Manitou in Québec where there are brook trout and a particular shiny variety of Arctic charr referred to as *Salvelinus nitidus* which the eskimos call *angmalook*. The reference to this fish is quite significant as JB wrote the Preface to the limited edition of the Canadian angling classic *Brown Waters* (1940) in which the author, W.H. Blake, describes it as the 'Malbaie' trout after the lake in which it is found.

Probably Buchan's most dedicated angler, appearing in many of his works, is Sir Edward Leithen whom many consider to be a self-portrait. Leithen picks up a rod whenever he has the opportunity, and two of opportunities appear in *The Gap in the Curtain* (1932):

> "I rose early and went for a walk along the Arm to look for a possible trout. The mayfly season was over, but there were one or two good fish rising beyond a clump of reeds where the stream entered the wood."

> "My sight is very good, especially for long distances and in dry-fly fishing I've never needed to use a glass to spot a fish. Well, in the little fishing I did that day, I found my eyes as good as ever, but I noted one remarkable defect. I saw the trout perfectly clearly, but I could not put a fly neatly over him. There was nothing wrong with my casting; the trouble was in my eye which had somehow lost its liaison with the rest of my body. The fly fell on the water as lightly as thistledown, but it was many inches away from the fish's nose."

Edward Leithen also figures in *John MacNab* (1925), where his particular task is to fish what many might consider the unfishable. However, his first appearance is in *The Power House* (1916). Even in this 'shocker' two references to fishing are slipped in on successive pages:

> "At that time I had a friend in one of the embassies, whose acquaintance I had made on a dry-fly stream in Hampshire .... Felix I found in the little library of the big secretaries' room, a sunburnt sportsman fresh from a Norwegian salmon river."

In *The Dancing Floor* (1926) a convalescent Leithen is shown round the estate by its undergraduate owner who remarks:

> "It's something to be able to see the hills from every window and to get a glimpse of the sea from the top floor. Goodish sport, too, for we've several miles of salmon and sea trout and we get uncommon high birds in the upper coverts."

He obviously enjoyed being with this young man and shared his enthusiasm for mutual interests for he says: "I have never taken to any one so fast as I took to that boy."

J.B.'s references to angling are endless, and while I would like to quote from them all I will leave the reader that pleasure. Sufficient it is perhaps to mention a few others briefly. In the well-known novel *Huntingtower* (1922) the provision merchant, Dickson McCunn, who had never fished in his life, chose the seventeenth-century classic *The Compleat Angler* to take on his hike because it 'seemed to fit his mood.' *The Half-Hearted* (1900) has a most appealing description of a girl's impressions as she walks by an upland trout stream and encounters two ragamuffins tickling trout and a young man, exasperated with his fishing tackle, whom she helps. This is something of a fantasy as, according to his second son, William, J.B.'s heroines are said to be a little unreal as women and are often relegated to little more than a decorative role.

With a list of over 100 titles to his pen it is not really surprising that some of the heroes are anglers when the author was one himself. Many of his short stories, collected together under such titles as *Scholar Gipsies* (1896), *Grey Weather* (1899) and the *Watcher by the Threshold* (1902), contain some delightful angling references. Ones that are likely to give particular pleasure are 'Politics and the Mayfly' in *Grey Weather* and 'Mayfly Fishing' in *Scholar Gipsies*.

To have read J.B.'s works one will have visited many places and fished many waters with a wide variety of interesting characters. The last verse of his Epilogue dedicated to Master Izaak Walton in his anthology *Musa Piscatrix* makes a fitting end to these travels:

> *Why weary with idle praise,*
> *Thou wanderer in Elysian ways?*
> *Where skies are fresh and fields are green,*
> *And never dust or smoke is seen,*
> *Nor news sheets, nor subscription lists,*
> *Nor merchants nor philanthropists,*
> *For these waters fall and flow*
> *By fragrant banks, and still below*
> *The great three-pounders rise and take*
> *The 'palmer', 'alder', 'dun' or 'drake',*
> *Now by that stream, if there you be,*
> *I prithee keep a place for me.*

Chapter 17 – **The Gorgeous Grayling**

Probably one of the most popular fish among anglers in Europe and North America after the trout and salmon is the grayling. Its soft, small rayless adipose fin just in front of its tail identifies it as a member of the salmon family which gives it an air of respectability. However, in other ways its attributes as a sporting fish may be something of an enigma. One feature it does have which I'm sure has something to do with its popularity is the possession of a very fine large and beautifully decorated dorsal fin. Whenever one sees an angler with his captured grayling he is always portrayed holding this fin spread out to its full size to demonstrate the one feature of the fish with which he is most pleased. At one time grayling were netted from rivers because they were considered vermin as they depleted the food supply of the more desirable trout and young salmon. There were of course some rivers where their presence was most welcome because, as they come into prime condition in the early autumn after their spring spawning, it enabled fishing to continue after trout were out of season and they could be taken on artificial fly as well as bait. The rivers of Derbyshire and Yorkshire came in this category, only in fairly recent years have the chalk stream anglers recognised the value of the grayling as a sporting fish. The formation of the Grayling Society, with a large and worldwide membership, has placed the grayling in its rightful place and where it receives the recognition it deserves.

In Yorkshire rivers such as the Ure, the Nidd and the Wharfe the grayling has always been a popular fish, and anglers such as Walbran and Pritt did much to extol their virtues in their books which are now angling classics.

It was on an autumn day the year the war ended that the bus from Harrogate dropped me at the bridge end in Summerbridge in Nidderdale. The sun was just burning the mist from the river and the surrounding fields and it promised to be a warm October day. Just upstream of the bridge, above the broken water there is a long pool. At that time there was a timber mill on the left tree-lined bank. Access was from the right bank and one could fish upstream to the islands unhindered. About 20 yards above the islands was a weir. Good trout lay between the weir and the islands. Grayling were rising all the way up the pool and most were lying close to the left bank. I had an 8½ft greenheart rod, a recent present from my parents, and a Hardy's Uniqua reel filled with a Kingfisher line well greased with Mucilin. Attached to this was a 9ft Hardy's tapered dry fly cast, well soaked overnight between two felt pads in an aluminium cast box. The choice of the fly was between a Sturdy's Fancy and a Grayling Witch. To me, a Sturdy's Fancy with its cream cock's hackle, peacock herl body and red wool tag, does best on a dull day and on fast water. The Grayling Witch seems better suited for bright days. The pale blue cock hackle, green peacock herl body ribbed with silver tinsel and red floss silk tag gives it a brightness for sunny occasions. So a Grayling Witch was tied on. As the fish were rising steadily along the length of the pool a systematic coverage of the river working steadily upstream was an easy decision. As there had been a frost already the fish should be more willing to take one's fly. In the summer months they would come to the surface and rise at one's fly but not take it. It was most frustrating particularly on some pools where they could be seen coming up from the river bed. However, today, grayling at the tail of the pool were soon being taken but

Two brace of Tweed grayling weighing 2½, 1¾, 1¾ and 1½lbs

were no more than 6 ounces and were released. Fortunately, as one went upstream they were of a more respectable size, reaching between 8 and 10 ounces, not large by chalkstream standards or of some larger northern rivers. Although a number of fish of between 1¼ and 2lb. were caught lower down the river at Killinghall and Knaresborough in 1945 and 1946. These were fish put in the river from Driffield Beck in East Yorkshire. By the time the top of the pool was reached a number of fish of ¾lb. had been added to the catch. Two or three slightly larger fish were caught between the islands and then some nice trout that were quickly returned. Just as I had finished, an angler came into the pool and started fishing with a float and maggot. Much to his surprise he had no success at all as he thought bait would be far more killing than fly, you never can tell! The sun had disappeared by lunch and, with a dozen fish to take home, I decided after a leisurely sandwich to walk down the river to find out how some friends fishing the Harrogate Flyfishers' Club water at Darley were faring. From there one could catch the Nidderdale train back to Harrogate. Beeching should never have been allowed to close these local branch lines, little did he know how much he was inconveniencing anglers.

Not all days grayling fishing were like the one just described. Usually one only caught three or four fish if one was lucky. By December it was trotting the red worm or maggot and early in the New Year rods were put away until the start of the trout season. If the weather was unseasonably warm grayling could be taken on the fly in December and a Sturdy's Fancy would often bring a fish to the surface.

The Ure, too, was a good grayling river, particularly in its upper reaches and Walbran, who sadly drowned in this river near Tanfield just upstream of Ripon, describes his time fishing for grayling with enthusiasm. There was one small area on the Ure much further downstream at Boroughbridge which grayling frequented. This was just below the weir among the islands, the home of splendid barbel, and just below the bridge over by the left bank. They were of a lovely colour with light olive to silver flanks, a very orange dorsal fin and plentifully spotted just behind the gill covers. They most closely resembled the picture of grayling in Travis Jenkins book *The Fishes of the British Isles both Fresh Water & Salt.*

Fishing with the nymph was a method not experienced until Richard and I went to fish the *Piscatorial Society's* waters on the Avon one October. The nymph used was the Sawyer Killer Bug or Grayling Bug tied by Frank Sawyer's wife. The Broads is a very good pool on the Society's water for grayling. It was a matter of using a floating line and casting upstream. As we were not skilled in detecting when fish had taken the nymph, even though we watched our lines carefully to try and detect any temporary halt in the line's drift downstream, a piece of white wool was tied on at the join of line and cast. It was very easy then to know when a fish had taken the nymph. The wool would stop and then move upstream as it submerged. It was then just a matter of striking and a grayling would be hooked. It was a lovely autumn day and soon we had lost count of the number of fish we'd caught and released. If the water had been clearer I'm sure we would have seen a shoal of released grayling swimming gracefully below us! The same method was used during a visit to the Wylye at Boyton. Here the water was much clearer and as one was almost on top of the fish they could be seen coming up between the fronds of water buttercup to intercept the nymph. Most of the fish caught were between 10 ounces and 1lb. It was most pleasant fishing these two chalk streams but the peace was spoilt by the incessant whine of traffic from the nearby motorway and at times the ear-piercing roar of jet aircraft from the nearby experimental air station at Boscombe Down.

The Tweed was one of those rivers from which grayling were netted because of the fear that they were having a detrimental effect on salmon and trout stocks. Tweed grayling grow to quite a respectable size as they do on its tributary the Teviot. There was a small core of anglers who fished for them in the winter after the salmon-fishing season was over, but to begin with there was some resistance to recognising grayling fishing as a legitimate sport as it was thought that the anglers were really after salmon or sea trout. Why any one should think this I cannot imagine, as salmon and sea trout kelts are not very appetising items. Reason is prevailing and the Tweed authorities now recognise that grayling fishing is an integral part of the local angling calendar. However, there has always been some part of Tweed where there was an enlightened attitude to grayling fishing.

It was two days after Christmas and Oliver Farr, the boatman at Rutherford, phoned to say that the river was in good order and would we like to come down for a spot of grayling fishing. We needed no second asking and the following day equipped with turkey sandwiches, Christmas cake and red worms, the latter for the fish, we were on our way to the Rutherford beat a few miles downstream of St. Boswells. Grayling need looking for on a big river and we tried the obvious places such as the head of pools where the current is slackening and especially in the eddies and then in the pools themselves where one might have to fish very deep. We used 10½ft. coarse fishing rods as the rod rings stand out preventing the 5lb. monofilament line from sticking to the rod itself. Fixed spool reels were chosen instead of centre pin ones, although my preference from days gone by is for the latter. Small red bob floats were chosen due to their easy visibility when trotting long distances.

There was a cold wind in the morning and fish were difficult to find but by lunchtime we each had two fish, all of them being caught about mid-day. At this time of year grayling are often caught just as its getting dark. There was one long pool with a good current coming in and an area of slack water on the right bank easily approached from a bank of gravel. This seemed a good spot on which to concentrate. A good flow of turbulent water entered the pool that shelved steeply into deep water. The technique was to cast up into the fast water and allow the bait to come into the slack and then drift down the pool in the calmer water at the side of the main current. At first the floats drifted unimpeded into the distance. Then, when the bait was cast slightly closer to the main current my float was pulled quickly down until it had almost disappeared from sight. On striking there was a strong resistance from a very heavy fish which turned out to be a lovely grayling of 1lb. 14oz. Richard followed and netted a specimen fish of 2lb. followed by one of 1lb. 14oz. More fish of similar weights followed the first two to the bank and providing we kept our baits in this rather confined zone we were guaranteed fish. If we were slightly outside this spot nothing happened. The light was failing fast and we were running out of worms, in fact we had to recycle them. Stumps were drawn as the last glimpse of daylight faded and the worms were exhausted. The eight fish kept ranged from 2lb. to 1lb. 6oz. and had a total weight of 14¼lb. An analysis of their stomachs as they were being cleaned for the table showed that they were all stuffed full of salmon eggs!

A similar experience with big Tweed grayling occurred some years later on the Middle Pavilion beat just below Melrose Bridge. It was mid-December and the river was running quite high, there had been a severe frost and the weather was extremely c-o-l-d and snow seemed imminent. As I wanted to try out my new J.W. Young Purist II centre pin reel I tackled up with a Bruce and Walker 10½ft. carbon fibre rod and put on an attractive red worm. The Elm Whiel was high but there was a good moderate flow at its head by the left bank. The reel was a delight and let the line out perfectly. On about the second run down this section of pool the float went under and I was into a very heavy fish. At first its weight and fight gave the impression of a small grilse or kelt and it kept boring out into the current. With a steady pressure the float came into view and then an enormous fin of a very large grayling. The fight was not over and for several minutes there was a heart-stopping tussle until it could be brought into the bank and netted. Would this make the magical 3lb., the ambition of every grayling angler? No, but its weight of 2½lb. made it an acceptable trophy. Further optimistic attempts to catch the hoped-for three pounder resulted in three more fish from the same spot weighing 1¾, 1¾ and 1½lb. Two hours had been spent on the river and that was quite long enough; especially as practically all feeling had gone from my hands and feet. Thoughts of a hot plate of soup were replacing all thoughts of more grayling and so I called it a day quite happily, after all, four grayling weighing 7½lbs. is nae bad.

Ross Gardiner of the Freshwater Fisheries Laboratory at Pitlochry and Scientific Officer of the Grayling Society kindly read the scales of the 2½lb. fish, which was a male and measured 44.45cm, and found it to be seven years old.

A local artist by the name of Bill Young kindly offered to paint the 2½lb. grayling in oils. So, rather than waste the fish I said he could have it to eat once he had made the necessary preliminary sketches. The painting is superb and hangs in our hall. Asking him for his opinion of the grayling's culinary attributes he said: "It was gorgeous and the best fish he'd ever eaten."

Chapter 18 – **A Spring Day in Ettrickdale**

It was a bright spring day with a cold wind, but black clouds on the horizon warned of the snow showers forecast. I was of two minds whether to go or not. It would be my first day's fishing of the season and it was now early May!

The weather held during the drive up the peaceful Ettrick valley so loved by James Hogg, the Ettrick shepherd, and his frequent companion Sir Walter Scott. Masses of primroses shone in the banks by the roadside lined with trees bearing new tender green leaves. Reaching the farm it was a drive along rough tracks to the loch through three or four fields.

It was hardly large enough to be called a man-made loch, more a man-made pond. A steep ditch discharged water from a diverted stream into the pond close to the outfall rather than the preferred furthest end, but the ever-present wind in this wild valley prevented any chances of stagnation. Conifers bordered two sides of the water, and a well-furnished wood-tiled hut at one end gave the angler sanctuary. The water had been stocked with rainbow trout and brook trout and was said to hold some browns from releases in past years. We should see.

A few fish were rising spasmodically where the trees came right down to the water's edge. Not wanting to use the small glass-fibre boat, a Hardy's 10ft. 3in. Fibalite Perfection rod with a 3in Sunbeam reel holding a sink-tip line was set up and a size 10 Viva lure was tied on to the cast. At least one could "search" the water with this traditional rainbow trout lure and see what happened. The Viva and Ace of Spades are two of the most successful lures for rainbows and browns on the still waters of southern and central Scotland at all times of the year. I only use them when there is little activity at the surface and only then to find out whether or not the fish are in a taking mood.

Once the line was sinking nicely the fly was retrieved slowly. At first a few desultory plucks and then something solid as the first rainbow of the day exploded at the surface and was brought fighting all the way to the net – a beautifully conditioned 2lb. silver fish with pronounced scarlet stripes along its flanks. Fish activity increased and sometimes fish took the fly as it was sinking and before retrieval had started. The first that one knew that a fish was interested was when the sinking line started to move away. At other times the fish would take the Viva in the momentary pauses during retrieving, so as one started to continue the retrieve one would feel a resistance which, of course, was a fish!

Eight good-conditioned rainbows between 1½lb and 2lb were taken in succession. They were almost certainly triploids, their three x-chromosomes guaranteeing almost 100% sterility so that energy went into making muscle rather than gonad production. Most were slipped back into the water to fight another day. Sport continued and, at last, the next three fish to come to the net were brown trout. Two would have each weighed 2lb. but, alas, although a lovely gold colour with big red and black spots, they were emaciated and virtually kelts and duly returned. Hopefully next time they were caught they would have fully recovered from their spawning in the inflowing ditch. The third brown was only a youngster, in lovely condition with perfect fins and, as none as small had ever been stocked, it was no doubt the progeny from local spawning.

It was some years since I had caught a brook trout so it was a delight to find that the next fish in the net was a brook. A pretty fish with a smooth dappled pink and green skin with minute red and blue spots. It is very like the arctic charr which is in the same genus, Salvelinus. The brook 'trout' is not a trout but a charr – *Salvelinus fontinalis* to taxonomists. Recently taxonomists, who love to change names, took the rainbow trout out of the genus Salmo, to which the Atlantic salmon and brown trout belong, and placed it with the Pacific salmon species which have the generic name Oncorhynchus. So we have the rainbow trout bearing the title *Oncorhynchus mykiss* in place of its previous label *Salmo gairdneri*.

By lunchtime the weather was beautifully warm and the willow warblers were singing and the curlews or whaups were calling on the nearby moor. It was almost hot in the shelter of the spruce trees and small black flies were landing on the water surface in some numbers and were enticing more fish to the surface. Determined not to be rushed, and after sandwiches and a snooze, a change was made to a floating line with a small greased black spider dressed on a size 16 hook tied to a fine leader. This is a reliable fly throughout the season as it represents the ubiquitous chironomid so abundant on still waters. This did the trick and two smaller rainbows and another brook trout came to the net. Although one could cast to a rising fish, which was most probably cruising, the more usual practice was to cast in the general direction of apparent fish activity and let the fly float at random, always keeping a straight line by retrieving slack as the fly is brought in with the waves.

Slowly sport eased, nothing more at the surface and no activity in the depths. The sun went behind the clouds and bird song ceased. It was time for tea.

Chapter 19 – **The Emerald Isle**

The Aer Lingus flight from Edinburgh arrived in Dublin on time and Martin O'Grady was there to meet me. He and Ken Whelan had arranged a week's fishing in various parts of Ireland and had very kindly asked me to join them. Ken was to meet up with is in couple of day's time. Martin and Ken both worked for the Central Fisheries Board so there was plenty to talk about on our first evening.

The following day Martin introduced me to Lough Ennell near Mulingar. The lough had had a nutrient enrichment problem, but this had been overcome and the trout stock was improving. The fishing method we were to use was completely new to me. It was dapping with a grasshopper using a floss silk line.. Martin motored up the lough and started a drift off one of the islands where there was some shelter from a fairly strong wind. The technique is to keep the grasshopper on top of the water. This is not easy when there are largish waves. One second the grasshopper is in the air and the next swimming for dear life under the water. Apparently the trout take the insect very quietly and almost sip the beast into their mouths. So the only indication that a fish has risen is the disappearance of the grasshopper and a small rise of little more than a ring, if that. One then has to have the presence of mind to recite the names of the Irish presidents and then strike. My grasshopper disappeared in the classical way but, only knowing the name of one Irish president, I struck too soon and there was only the slightest resistance and the fish was away. That was that and there was no more interest shown in our little friends. Martin noticed a flock of black-headed gulls flying around an area of the loch some distance away and diving on to the surface periodically. This suggested a local hatch of flies and perhaps a rise of fish. We therefore motored down to investigate and changed over to conventional flies, one of them being the popular Green Peter. The gulls had dispersed by the time we arrived and there was no sign of fish. We kept at it for quite a while longer but, as there was no fish activity, we called it a day.

The following day Ken joined us and we gave our grasshoppers a bath on Loch Owel (pronounced ool). It was very windy and our drifts were very fast. However, trout came to the grasshoppers and we all caught fish. I managed two of between 12 ounces and 1lb. and was pleased to have mastered fishing with "live" bait. David Piggins and I used the same technique on Loch Cara but with daddy-long-legs. However, it was a windless day and the daddies looked pretty sad and the trout showed no interest in them. The highlight of that day was pulling up on the shore and having lunch with our wives and making tea with a Kelly's kettle.

Our next destination was Connemara. It was a wet and windy day when we reached Clifden or thereabouts and there was no rush to get out on the lough. After a prolonged lunch we risked it and fished loughs Lurgeen and Invermore. Most of the time was spent fishing from the shore and three sea trout came to my Connemara Black. Ken and Martin, along with Paddy Gargan who was over there for the summer, had similar success. It was hard work and we were all glad to reach our base for the night.

The reputation of the River Erriff was well-known, not least from write-ups in *Trout and Salmon*. It was therefore a great treat to arrive there late the following morning after a tour of Connemara to show me the good sea trout loughs. It was a beautiful day, the wind had dropped and it promised to be a rewarding day. I couldn't wait to get on the bank. I love the Irish, they are a warm-hearted and generous people, but when they start talking they lose all sense of time. So it was today. On arrival at the lodge, where all the anglers stayed, there was a general catching up with the news with the lodge steward and a resident biologist. Then we had to have coffee and then more talk. It was now lunchtime, but no sign of lunch nor of movement to the river. At last someone thought that perhaps we should be away fishing. My digestive system by now had lost all track of time and I ignored its rumblings and tackled up feverishly. Unfortunately the only salmon rod I brought with me was a Bruce and Walker 10½ft. carbon fibre grilse/sea trout rod which I thought would be adequate, but another foot or so would have been better and would have enabled one to fish the pools more effectively. I put on a Red Fox, a pattern new to me, and started at the top of the Quarrie Pool. About half way down the fly was taken fiercely and the fish gave quite a tussle. It was therefore quite a surprise to land a rather emaciated 2¾lb. sea trout. Ken did no better but the other anglers who had been out all day had fared pretty well.

The party of anglers at the Lodge were nearly all from the Welsh Water Authority at the invitation of the Central Fisheries Board and among them was Gareth Edwards who is as good a salmon angler as he was a rugby player. The following morning we were allocated beats and I was to fish below the Aasleagh Falls, which seemed a good bet. However, although fish were moving through none took an interest in my fly. Looking back, a fly fished on a riffle hitch might have been successful. The day remained a frustrating blank and all the time the wish was for a longer rod, but it was a beautiful day and one couldn't have seen Co. Galway under better conditions. One word of warning if visiting the Irish west coast, and it was a warning given me by a resident, keep to the Guinness and leave the tap water alone. It can play havoc with your insides, as I learnt to my cost!

Our final venue was the Burrishoole Fishery run by David Piggins the Director of the Salmon Research Trust for Ireland and a great friend of mine for many years. The Welsh Water Authority was out here in force. Chris Mills on the staff of the Salmon Research Trust acted as my amiable boatman and had us fleeing across Lough Furnace in no time. It was an overcast day and the lough was pretty calm. A few sea trout were rising and we had two in the boat at 1½lb. and 12oz. on a Jungle Bunny and a Delphi. Very few grilse were caught that day. It had been a super week and the Irish hospitality was tremendous and Martin and Ken were excellent hosts.

The next Irish experience was again courtesy of Ken and also Paddy Gargan who at that time was in charge of the Galway Fishery. This time we were to fish the Corrib on the Galway Fishery. Ken met the flight at Knock and we then drove down to Newport on a glorious day in late May. Ken was now Director of the Salmon Research Trust of Ireland, having taken over after the retiral of David Piggins. We spent the evening enticing small trout on a neighbouring lough and the following day drove down to Galway where we met Ken's brother, Brendan and his father, Jimmy just in time for the afternoon shift on the river. Jackie Charlton had been fishing there in the morning and, being the coach for the Irish football team, half of Galway was on the bridge watching him fish. The crowd moved on as we took to the water.

It's not an easy stretch of river to fish. The river pours over a weir and an array of sluices. Wading on the left bank is difficult because of large stones and boulders and a fairly long cast is required. Fishing from the right bank is from

The happy Whelans: Ken, Jimmy and Brendan

a high wall for about half the length of the beat down to the bridge and then a less steep section from there to the bridge. Casting with a fly rod is difficult because of a wall and high ground behind and it requires a good Spey cast or a less conventional steeple cast to get the line well out to the centre of the river. A cast across the river at right angles to the bank makes it slightly easier than casting diagonally downstream. Fish had been caught in the morning but there was less activity in the afternoon. Although we were fishing fly, all legal angling methods are permitted and many anglers fish with shrimp and prawn even though fish are taking fly at the time. Perhaps it is the difficult casting that makes them prefer to fish more easily with bait. A number of flies are recommended including Goldfinch, Lemon Grey, Thunder and Lightning, Silver Doctor, Hairy Mary and Shrimp. While fishing the right bank with a shrimp fly I noticed a little man sitting on the grass watching me. He was a tiny man and looked almost like what I thought a leprechaun should be. We got into conversation and his Irish brogue fascinated me. He admired my 13-foot Sharpe's spliced impregnated cane rod and asked what fly I was using. He asked if I'd tried a Garry Dog. No, I hadn't any. "Well", he said "it so happens

I have some" and took out a small box containing a number of Garry Dogs tied on size 10 and 12 trebles and handed me some. I was most grateful and my attention was diverted while admiring the beautiful way they'd been tied and putting them in my fly box. On looking up to thank him once more I couldn't see him anywhere. He'd vanished into thin air. I thought it strange but felt he was a little embarrassed by enthusiasm for the way the flies had been tied and had gone on up the path by the river.

Shortly after this encounter we finished fishing for the day and headed into Galway for a meal. It was arranged that all four of us would go down to the river before breakfast and then take it in turns for two of us at a time to go back to the B&B for a late breakfast. It was a lovely sunny morning and a large shoal of grilse could be seen in the centre of the pool sheltering among the rocks. They must have entered the pool recently, as there had been no sign of them yesterday. We were all fishing from the right bank. One of the little man's Garry Dogs was tied on and I cast out towards the grilse shoal. My line

A 12lb sea trout from the Tweed at Melrose. The fish has lost its sea colouration having been in fresh water for a few weeks. These large Tweed sea trout were referred to as 'bull trout' by early salmon biologists.

tightened and a fish was on and fought energetically. Landing a fish on the right bank involved help from another angler, as one had to lead the fish down the river below the wall to where the bank was less steep and get to a platform where a massive net with a long heavy handle was lying. Trying to net a fish with this instrument one-handed was virtually impossible. It required two arms to lift the net with a fish in its embraces. Ken was there to help and a 6lb. grilse was on the bank. Shortly after another 6lb. grilse took the Garry Dog and the same performance was repeated. Then it was Ken's turn to bring a fish to the platform and mine to net it. Then a grilse of 5lb. took the Garry Dog and another was lost. By now it was time for breakfast with three grilse on the bank to my rod and two grilse to Ken's and one to Brendan's. Brendan and Jimmy caught more fish after breakfast. Other rods had been taking fish but mostly on shrimp and prawn. Paddy Gargan appeared during the proceedings and was visibly delighted at our luck and was intrigued with the Garry Dogs. The morning was over all too soon and sadly it was now a drive back to Knock. Ireland looked beautiful from the air and everything was emerald green. I fished the little man's Garry Dog again some time later and caught my largest ever sea trout of 12lb. with it. Who says there's no such thing as fairies?!

Chapter 20 – **Scott on Salmon**

Introduction to the works of Sir Walter Scott at school always tended to be deadly dull. What a difference it would have made if our masters had only led off by telling us that this poet and writer of good stories was not only a member of the legal profession and a sheriff, but also a country sportsman and an angler and had poacher's instincts.

Scott was no part-timer in country pursuits and John Buchan in his biography of Scott says:

"Scott liked to be ten hours a day in the open air, shooting, fishing, coursing and riding, a 'rattle-skulled half lawyer', half sportsman as he called himself. In fishing he was no great performer in the orthodox parts, as he declares in his review of Sir Humphrey Davy's *Salmonia* that his (fishing) line usually fell (on the water) 'with the emphasis of a quoit'. However, we must be grateful that he pursued the gentle art as, in searching through his fishing tackle on one occasion to find some items for a friend, he came across his long-lost incomplete draft of *Waverley.*"

This modesty for his skill as an angler surfaces elsewhere, and in his Preface to the 1821 edition of Richard Franck's *Northern Memoirs* when he, in quoting a verse by the poet John Richards, refers to himself as being: "No fisher but a well wisher to the game." Although John Purdie, a nephew of Scott's general factotum Tom Purdie, had this to say of Scott's angling ability: "….young Sir Walter was gude wi' aither rod or leister – a better never threw a line …. Ah me! I can see him now throw his line wi' a 16lb rod across the Carey Weel pool and make her licht like a feather at the far side."

Scott loved to 'burn the water' of an autumn night when the salmon were 'turning up their sides like swine'. On such occasions he was as much in the river as out of it. Burning the water entailed a foray to the river at night when salmon were plentiful using a torch of burning peat or coal, referred to as a 'blaze', to illuminate the water and, when a salmon was sighted, to spear the fish using a leister or waster. This implement consisted of a wooden shaft attached by a socket to an arrangement of barbed iron prongs numbering from one to seven, not unlike Neptune's trident. With the passing of the Tweed Act of 1857 the leister was banned and the Tweed Amendment Act of 1859 made it an offence to be in possession of such an implement within five miles of the river. Prior to that time leistering was often a social event and one in which Sir Walter delighted to participate. James Hogg talks of him being in his highest glee when 'toiling in Tweed to the waist' with rod or leister. Jamie relates to him while he lived at Ashestiel:

"He and Skene of Rubislaw and I were out one night, about midnight, leistering kippers *(a term given to spawning fish, particularly male or cock fish because of their reddish-brown colouration)* in Tweed, and on going to kindle a light at the Elibank March, we found, to our inexpressible grief, that our coal had gone out. To think of giving up our sport was out of the question; so we had no other shift to send Rob Fletcher home, all the way through the darkness, the distance of two miles, for another fiery peat ... Rob Fletcher came at last, and Mr. Laidlaw of Peel with him, and into the foaming river we plunged, in our frail bark, with a blazing light. In a few minutes we came to Gliddy's Weal, the deepest pool in Tweed, when we perceived that our bark gave evident symptoms of sinking. When Scott saw the terror Peel was in, he laughed till the tears blinded his eyes. Always the more mischief, the better sport for him. "For God's sake push he to the side!" roared Peel. 'Oh she goes fine,' said Scott; 'An gin the boat were bottomless, an' seven miles to row;' and by the time we got out the words, down she went to the bottom, plunging us all into Tweed over head and ears. It was no sport to me at all; but that was a glorious sight for Sir Walter, and the next day he was no worse."

It was this experience and discomfort of spearing salmon, which I'm sure led to the inclusion of a vivid and detailed account of the pursuit in *Guy Mannering*:

"Ground the waster weel, man! Ground the waster weel! – haud him down – ye hae nae the pith o' a cat!" – were the cries of advice, encouragement, and expostulation, from those who were on the bank, to the sportsman engaged with the salmon, who stood up to his middle in water, jingling among broken ice, struggling against the force of the fish and the strength of the current, and dubious in what manner he should attempt to secure his booty ... instead of advancing his light, the friend let it drop in the water. "The deil's in Gabriel!" said the spearman, as the fragments of glowing wood floated half blazing, half sparkling, but soon extinguished, down the stream – "the deil's in the man! – I'll never master him without the light – and a braver kipper, could I but land him, never reisted abune a pair of cleeks". Some dashed into the water to lend their assistance, and the fish, which was afterwards found to weigh nearly thirty pounds, was landed in safety."

The fish were not caught for personal gain, as would be the case nowadays, but for distribution among the community:

"The sportsmen returned loaded with fish, upwards of one hundred salmon having been killed within the range of their sport. The best were selected for the use of the principal farmers; the others divided among their shepherds, cottars, dependants, and others of inferior rank who attended. These fish, dried in the turf smoke of their cabins, or shealings, formed a savoury addition to the mess of potatoes mixed with onions, which were the principal part of their winter food."

Leistering, although it was not illegal at that time, gave Scott an affinity with poaching. When a well-known Darnick poacher by the name of Tom Purdie came before him at Selkirk Sheriff Court he took a liking to him and, when he was acquitted on some formality, he made him his factotum and guardian, a position he held until his death. However, he was hard on poachers if needs be and in his *Journal* for 1830 he refers to being obliged to hold a black fishing court (*black fish are fish that have just finished spawning and are known as kelts*) at Selkirk. As he says, this was not a popular matter, as salmon did not get up to the upper reaches of the river (*the Ettrick*) during the fishing season, and were only there in numbers during spawning time. They were therefore only available to the locals when they were 'out of season'. So that for several years during the end of the year the 'gentry':

"finding no advantage from preserving the spawning fish, neglected the matter altogether in a kind of dudgeon, and the peasantry laid them waste at their will. As the property is very valuable, the proprietors down the country agreed to afford some passage for the fish when the river (*fishing season*) is open, providing they will protect the fish during the close time. A new Act has been passed, with heavy penalties and summary powers of recovery. Some persons are cited under it today; and a peculiar licence of poaching having always distinguished the district of late years, we shall be likely to have some disturbance."

Scott goes on to say that: "Six black fishers were tried, four were condemned. All went very quietly until the conclusion, when one of the criminals attempted to break out. I stopped him for the time with my own hand." An account of this incident is given by an eye-witness, Mr. Peter Rodger, Procurator-Fiscal, who says: "The prisoner, thinking it a good chance to escape, made a movement in the direction of the door. This Sir Walter detected in time to descend from the bench and place himself in the desperate man's path. 'Never!' said he; 'if you do, it will be over the body of an old man.' Whereupon other officials of the Court came to the Sheriff's assistance and the prisoner was secured."

Having such a close involvement with salmon poaching in his role as a country sheriff, it is not surprising that reference to the fisheries laws appears from time to time in his novels. In *The Antiquary*, Oldbuck, in discussing the origin of the term *salmon-length* with Lovel, remarks: "You are aware that the space allotted for the passage of salmon through a dam, dike or weir, by statute, is the length within which a full-grown pig can turn himself round." This is a reference to Salmon Acts passed in the time of David I (1124-1153) and of William the Lion (1164-1214).

Fishing expeditions with Scott were sociable events and the party would feast by the waterside on fresh-caught salmon boiled in their broo. Scott had many friends who enjoyed salmon fishing, one of whom was Sir Humphrey Davy author of *Salmonia*. Lockhart , Scott's son-in-law, portrays a delightful picture of the 'illustrious inventor of the safety-lamp': "His fisherman's costume, a brown hat with flexible brims, surrounded with line upon line of catgut and innumerable flyhooks, jackboots worthy of a Dutch smuggler, and a fustian jacket dabbled with blood of salmon, made a fine contrast with the smart jackets, white cord breeches, and well-polished jockey boots of the less distinguished cavaliers about him."

The reaches of Tweed most frequently fished by Scott were those of Charlie Purdie at Boldside and his neighbour, Lord Somerville, situated just upstream of Melrose Bridge and now known as Upper Pavilion. The latter boasts such well-known pools as Carey Wheel, Brig End (the one-time site of a toll bridge mentioned in *The Monastery*) and Meg's Hole – the pool in which Black Meg of Darnick drowned and who now frequents the water in the form of a heron or cormorant. A tale recounted at length by William Scrope in *Days and Nights of Salmon Fishing in the Tweed.*

References to salmon angling do not go amiss in his novels. In *Quentin Durward*, King Louis XI of France in reply to Oliver says: "I am an old experienced salmon, and use not to gulp the angler's hook because it is busked with a feather called honour."

Several references to salmon angling appear in *St. Ronan's Well,* a story set in Tweeddale. Some of the characters are from time to time involved in small wagers, particularly when Squire Mowbray and Sir Bingo Binks of the Claret Club were around:

"I say little Sir Bingo," said the Squire, "this is the very fellow that we saw down at the Willow-slack on Saturday – he was tog'd gnostically enough, and cast twelve yards of line with one hand – the fly fell like thistledown on the water."

"We saw him pull out the salmon yonder," said Mowbray, "you remember – clean fish – the tide ticks on his gills – weighed I dare say, a matter of eighteen pounds."

If by 'tide ticks' Squire Mowbray meant tide- or sea-lice they would not be on the fish's gills. However, if by tide ticks he meant gill maggots the fish would have been a kelt, a baggot or a previous spawner. The life history of the salmon gill maggot (*Salmincola salmonea*) was not known in Scott's time and was only unravelled in 1941 by G.F. Friend in the Department of Zoology at Edinburgh University. However, no doubt Scott was referring to sea lice (*Lepeophtheirus salmonis)* which occurs on the body of the salmon and, occasionally, on the gill covers. These indicate that the salmon is newly in from the sea and therefore in good condition. If the salmon was caught in the vicinity of St. Ronan's Well, which one assumes is Innerleithen, then it is very unlikely that salmon would still bear tide lice. These die and fall off the fish within two or three days of entering fresh water. Rarely do salmon ascend as far as Innerleithen in such a short space of time.

Sir Bingo was not to be outdone and wrote to the angler involved:

"Sur – Jack Moobray has betted with me that the salmon you killed on Saturday last weyd ni to eighteen pounds, - I say nyer sixteen. So, you being a spurtsman, 'tis refer'd ... Postscript – Have sent some loops of Indian gout, also some black hakkels of my groom's dressing; hope they will prove killing, as suiting river and season."

Black hakkels figured prominently in the dressings of quite a few Tweed salmon flies at that time, including Kinmont Willie, The Lady of Mertoun, Toppy and Michael Scott.

Scott's interest in the natural history of salmon, as is apparent from his reference to 'tide ticks', was probably stimulated by his discussions with Sir Humphry Davy and William Scrope, author of *Days and Nights Salmon Fishing on the Tweed*. Scrope at that time was tenant of the Pavilion near Melrose and owned by Lord Somerville, and was a frequent visitor to Abbotsford, as was Scott to the Pavilion. In his *Journals* Scott remarks:

"This day we went to dinner at Mr. Scrope's at the Pavilion where were the Haigs of Bemerside, Isaac Haig, Mr. and Mrs. Bainbridge, etc. Warm dispute whether parr are or are not salmon trout."

There had been some controversy whether parr were the young of salmon. Scrope had demonstrated that if one scraped the silvery scales off the seaward migrating salmon smolts the livery of the parr was exposed. It was later confirmed on higher authority that the parr was indeed the young of the salmon. Scott, as he so often did, brought this acquired knowledge into his novels. In this instance it appears in *The Abbot*, when Mary, Queen of Scots, remarks to Roland Graeme on the high flavour and beautiful red colour of the Loch Leven trouts. She enquires into the place where the fish had been taken, their size, their peculiarities and a comparison between the Loch Leven trouts and those which are found in the lakes (yes, Scott actually says 'lakes') and rivers of the south of Scotland. Graeme starts a dissertation on 'Loch Leven trout, and sea trout, and river trout, and bull trout and char which never rise to a fly, and par, which some suppose infant salmon.'

Some of the controversial issues involving salmon today were subjects of concern even in Scott's time, particularly netting. In *Redgauntlet* an apparently legal and sporting method of catching salmon in the Solway was spearing on horseback:

"The scene was animated by the exertions of a number of horsemen, who were actually employed in hunting salmon;….they chased the fish at full gallop, and struck them with their barbed spears, as you see hunters spearing boars in the old tapestry. The salmon, to be sure, take things more quietly than the boars; but they are so swift in their own element , that to pursue and strike them is the task of a good horseman, with a quick eye, a determined hand, and full command of both his horse and weapon. The shouts of the fellows as they galloped up and down in the animating exercise – their loud bursts of laughter when any of their number caught a fall – and still louder acclamations when any of the party made a capital stroke with his lance – gave so much animation to the whole scene."

No doubt this description was enlivened by his own attempts at harpooning salmon on Tweed!

These same 'sportsmen' were literally in arms against the new tide-nets that prevented fish from entering the Solway rivers, as is most clear from Redgauntlet's remarks to the quaker netsman, Joshua Geddes:

"So, ho! Friend Joshua – thou art early to the road this morning. Has the spirit moved thee and thy righteous brethren to act with some honesty, and pull down yonder tide-nets that keep the fish from coming up the river?"

"Surely, friend, not so," answered Joshua firmly, but good-humouredly at the same time; "thou cans't not expect that our own hands should pull down what our own purses established. Thou killest the fish with spear, line and coble net; and we with snares and with nets, which work by the ebb and flow of the tide. Each doth what seems best in his eyes to secure a share of the blessing which Providence hath bestowed on the river, and that within his own bounds. O, prithee seek no quarrel against us, for thou shalt have no wrong at our hand."

How delightful! I wonder if our present day netsmen would speak so politely? Anyway, Redgauntlet was having none of it:

"Be assured I will take none at the hand of any man, whether his hat be cocked or broad-brimmed," answered the fisherman. "I tell you in fair terms, Joshua Geddes, that you and your partners are using unlawful craft to destroy the fish in the Solway by stake nets and wears; and that we, who fish fairly, and like men, as our fathers did, have daily less sport and less profit. Do you think gravity or hypocrisy can carry it off as you have done? The world knows you, and we know you. You will destroy the salmon which make the livelihood of fifty poor families, and then wipe your mouth, and go to make a speech at Meeting."

History repeats itself! Only we have more peaceful ways of curtailing netting than in those days. Redgauntlet continues:

"I give you fair warning, we will be upon you one morning soon, when we will not leave a stake standing in the pools of the Solway: and down the tide they shall every one go, and well if we do not send a lessee along with them."

This was no idle threat and was shortly executed, as we learn from the Provost:

"You must know – indeed I think you must have heard, that the fishermen at Brokenburn, and higher up the Solway, have made a raid upon quaker Geddes's stake-nets and levelled all with the sands."

"In troth I heard it, Provost, and I was glad to hear the scoundrels had so much pluck left, as to right themselves against a fashion which would make the upper heritors a sort of clocking hens, to hatch the fish that the folks below them were to catch and eat."

How familiar this last point is among anglers presently, and now with some success, endeavouring to have the north-east England salmon drift-net fishery closed!

There is no doubt that Sir Walter had his heart in the right place and, although he enjoyed pursuing salmon with a spear and harpoon one can be sure that he preferred rod and line, as is clear from a verse in his poem *On Ettrick's Mountains Dun:*

> *Along the silver streams of Tweed,*
> *'Tis blithe the mimic fly to lead*
> *When to the hook the salmon springs*
> *And the line whistles through the rings:*
> *The boiling eddy see him try,*
> *Then dashing from the current high,*
> *Till watchful eye and cautious hand,*
> *Have led his wasted strength to land.*

Chapter 21 – **Tweed's Largest Salmon**

This amusing and fictitious account of the capture of what was reputed to be Tweed's largest salmon has been extracted from the Edinburgh Angling Club Records for April, 22nd, 1875.

"The circumstances that I am about to relate are so extraordinary, and the adventure altogether so marvellous, that were it not that the truth of the details can be vouched for by the unimpeachable testimony of several gentlemen, I should hesitate ere I wrote this account. The whole proceeding, however, was witnessed by: William Menzies, Sec., A.Z. Usher, R.G. Trail, A. Hamilton, I. McWhirter, Robert Hardie and George Martin, who will one and all depose on their oaths to the truth of the statement.

Last night, April 21, I retired to bed about midnight and shortly after remembered that Robert had spoke of having seen a Royal salmon in the Bridge Pool, and that I had made arrangements to attempt the capture of this uncommon fish on the following morning. Just on the point of starting, I was distressed beyond measure to find that some villain in the Nest (*the headquarters of the Edinburgh Angling Club*) had destroyed a perfectly new white chimney pot hat of mine (*a headgear frequently worn by Edinburgh Angling Club members*), a hat of superior description and worth at least 25/-. The annoyance was so great that I determined to give up the project, but at that moment Russel (*one-time editor of* The Scotsman) who had just come from the bar of the House of Commons, drove up to the front of The Nest with his four greys, good temper being restored, the whole party got into the drag and we soon reached the Bridge Pool.

Here I was at work with Hamilton's American rod, a small lithe weapon, made of 24573 pieces of bamboo, interlaced with silver wire which cost £300. For the first time in his life Robert was nervous, indeed his trepidation was so painful it was necessary to keep him up to the mark with several drams of Glenlivet. His last words to me were: "Man if ye get the fush and no' kill him, ye'll go to Hell as sure as I'm standing before ye." I used the lightest hair tackle and a bright green midge. At the third cast I raised the monster and at the fourth cast amidst the most intense excitement of the onlookers I had him firm. "For God's sake haud the top o your rod up and gie him line" shouted Robert. Away he went slowly at first but soon increasing his paces he dashed madly up and down the Pool lashing the whole of the Pool into froth and covering the party on the bank with foam. Then he took to jumping, about 20 feet in the air at first, but soon increasing this in his mad desire to get rid of the green midge. He rose higher and higher until at last he threw himself into the air at least 50 feet perpendicular, Robert came up staggering "Man" he said, solemnly and slowly, "Ye have done a wicked act in fushing for this Royal Fush, but if he jumps again, let go your line as you value your soul, fer he'll be ower the bridge as sure as my name's Robert." With that he fainted clean away. But he was right. With a supreme effort, the monster propelled himself from the Pool, rose like a comet into the air and shot clear across the bridge and dashed into the water on the other side with a sound like thunder and sped up the stream at a terrible pace. Luckily I had 1000 yards of line but this would have been of little avail had not Menzies (who by the way was the only man who kept his head clear during the fight), come to my aid.

He at that moment spied the train coming along from Clovenfords. To stop the train, jump on the engine and push on to Clovenooks was the work of a moment. Seizing a small bottle of sewage he dashed down to the river and was just in time to uncork it and throw it into midstream before the monster arrived. The effect was magical, he paused, turned, and presently came downstream again to the bridge.

All this time my line had never slackened, and now it was evident he was preparing for another jump over the bridge. This was his last jump in life. Up he rose splendidly and slowly but just in mid-air a well-aimed shot from Captain McWhirter's rifle sent an ounce bullet through his body and he fell dead into the pool, which he had just left five hours before.

He was a clean run fish with sea-lice on him and he weighed exactly 2 cwts. (*224lbs*)."

Chapter 22 – **History of Scottish Angling Clubs**

<u>Piscator</u> - *I am (Sir) a Brother of the Angle, and you are to note*
that we Anglers all love one another.
(<u>Compleat Angler</u>), 1653).

Although the gentle art of angling, the contemplative man's recreation, is considered by most to be a solitary pastime in which the participant can quietly commune with nature, man, being naturally gregarious, hankers after company. It is therefore not surprising that the angler, in the course of time that has elapsed since the writings of Dame Juliana Berners, Izaak Walton and William Samuels, sixteenth century author of the *Arte of Angling,* has formed clubs and associations to this end. Such social units allow him to have his fishing organised, his aprés-fishing functions arranged and enable him to pit his skill against colleagues for coveted prizes.

The first club of this sort to be formed in Scotland was the *Ellem Fishing Club* in Duns, Berwickshire. Started in 1829 by a small number of Edinburgh and Berwickshire gentlemen it has become one of the best-known angling clubs in the country. It started in a small way when, at the first annual general meeting in 1830 held at the Ellem Fishing Tavern, the eleven original members signed the Articles of the Constitution and on the same day admitted three renowned local anglers to membership. The original members thought that there should only be admission of a member subject to a test of his skill as an angler.

Four years later, in 1834, the *West of Scotland Piscatorial Club* was born at a meeting of its first six members at the Waterloo Tavern in Glasgow. One of the first rules in the Constitution of this body was 'that members must be persons who are known to be lovers of piscatorial amusements', although nowhere is a 'piscatorial amusement' defined.

The well-known *Edinburgh Angling Club* was the next to appear on the scene in 1847 followed by the *Perth Anglers' Club* in 1854. Then, between 1858 and the turn of the century, at least forty more clubs were established, most of them using hotels and taverns as their meeting places.

With the advent of so many clubs it was only a matter of time before they organised themselves into an even larger body and it is therefore not surprising that a Scottish National Angling Clubs Association was formed in 1880. It was not until 1892 that this association had a constitution and two of the objects of the association were (1) to promote excellence in the art of angling by means of artificial fly-fishing with a single rod and line for the capture of trout and salmon and (2) to affiliate clubs in England, Ireland and Scotland, and to promote friendship among members of the angling clubs which are members of this association. The Association went from strength to strength and, with the rapid increase in angling activity in Scotland since the 1900s there were soon about 160 member clubs. Many more angling clubs than this occur in Scotland and a conservative estimate would put the number at 200.

Before looking at the activities of some of these clubs it is of interest to scan the rules as, like the small print on an insurance policy, they are usually taken for granted and therefore rarely read in their entirety. An interesting provision in the original Articles of Constitution of the *Ellem Fishing Club* was one that stipulated that every member should attend the Annual General Meeting and absence would result in a fine of half a guinea unless he provided the secretary on the day prior to the meeting with a certificate from a physician or surgeon stating that he was not in a fit state to attend. To enforce this rule the club appointed a Dr. Stewart of Duns to be the Medical Officer of the club but, alas, the doctor was fined for not competing in the angling competitions and, on being told the decision, he curtly replied that he thought his position was an honorary one and that he had no taste for the gentle art. The rules of the West of Scotland Piscatorial Club required members to meet on the first Tuesday of each month and 'each member will be fined one shilling unless a sufficient apology is given.' An interesting rule, which still divides the professional from the amateur in many branches of sport, is one applying to the *Gala Angling Association* which excludes from its membership any person who maintains himself solely by fishing.

It is a common practice for efficiently organised bodies of people to adorn themselves in some way so as to provide instant recognition among members.

This is taken to its extreme in regiments of soldiers in full dress uniform. Self-adornment in anglers is not a well-developed practice, but a desire for some form of traditional dress, as in the fox-hunting field, led the *Ellem Fishing Club* to emulate another Border club, the *Tweeddale Shooting Club,* in having a dress for social functions. The anglers decided upon a dark green dress coat, double-breasted of course, with the skirt lined with silk of the same colour. The club button on the collar to be of the same cloth as the coat. A buff vest, also with the club button, black trousers and white silk stockings completed the ensemble and thus closely resembled the dress of the *Tweeddale Shooting Club.* The *West of Scotland Piscatorial Club* considered a uniform in 1855 but, as tastes were various, the idea was abandoned. A Button Committee, however, decided upon a button having a fish hook in the centre with the name of the club around it. Unfortunately, the patternmaker was unable to get such a long name around the button so he shortened the name to the *West of Scotland Angling Club.* The club had therefore to change its name! Most clubs go to less trouble. A few, such as the *Phoenix* in Glasgow, have a badge and a tie, but others, and then only a handful, have simply a tie but this is expected to be worn at all angling functions.

The main purpose of angling clubs is to have fishing available for its members and to compete with one another for trophies and prizes, and to this end competitions are organised both between members of the same club and also with members of other clubs. Some clubs have their own fishing waters or lease them from riparian owners, but most of the city clubs have no fishings of their own and must book it on waters belonging to others. For this reason many fish on large waters such as Loch Leven or have outings to rivers where public fishing is available by ticket. The *Kelso Angling Club* and the *County of Peebles Angling Improvement Association* come into the first category and enjoy fishing on some miles of Tweed which is leased to them at a nominal rent by farmers and estates. Into the second category come the *Edinburgh Walton, Mid-Lothian* and *Phoenix, which* have most of their outings on Loch Leven. Some clubs are well provided for and the *Edinburgh Angling Club* has leased since its early days a stretch of Tweed near Ashestiel where its headquarters in the shape of a delightful cottage called the *Robin's Nest* was sited. Alas, it is no longer their property. Other clubs have always had to travel some distance to reach their fishing. It is difficult to picture the trials of reaching one's fishing grounds before the fast car and motorway. For the first fifteen years of the *West of Scotland Angling Club's* life there was no railway connection between Glasgow and the upper reaches of the Clyde. Members were compelled to go to fish either by mail coach or on horseback or to drive a horse and trap. As most members lived north of the Clyde and, in fact, almost next door to the Black Bull Hotel in Glasgow from which the mail coaches left, the mail coach was very popular. In 1850, however, the Caledonian Railway had moved its Glasgow terminus to Buchanan Street and the train was therefore more readily available to club members. This club also used to fish the River Echaig, which flows into the north shore of the Firth of Clyde near Kilmuir close to Dunoon. In 1834 the Post Office Directory listed no fewer than 29 vessels which sailed from Broomielaw to all parts of the Firth and round the coast. Boards enumerating their departure were to be seen at the Post Office Cross and below the Piazza of the Exchange. All were vessels under 100 tons, paddle-driven with a tall funnel centrally rigged. Even when the West of Scotland members went to fish the River Dochart in Perthshire, which flows into the upper end of Loch Tay, they would leave by steamer from Broomielaw, connecting with another steamer on Loch Lomond. On reaching Luib at the upper end of the loch they still had an appreciable journey ahead of them before they reached their destination at Crianlarich.

The east of Scotland clubs, particularly those with their headquarters in Edinburgh, had much easier journeys. There were frequent trains to the Borders and anglers could alight at any of the numerous stations along Tweed and Gala Water. The publication of *The Border Angler* in 1858, "a guide book to the Tweed and its tributaries and the other streams commanded by the North British Railway" was invaluable to Edinburgh anglers. Going north, the North British Railway Company issued a 3/6d return fare to Kinross by Loch Leven on the 6.05a.m. train from Waverley returning at 7.15 p.m. Such an early start and late finish to the day's proceedings prompted many clubs to order breakfast and dinner for participants at the Bridgend Hotel in Kinross. Some clubs, such as the *Midlothian* even to this day still strive to maintain the tradition of a dinner at the Bridgend after the day's fishing.

Ever since the late 1850s Loch Leven has probably been the most popular venue with all central Scotland angling clubs. It is a big sheet of water and, at least over the hundred or so years ending in the late 1970s, had a large population of presentable brown trout whose future was provided by a number of pollution-free spawning streams. It is easily accessible and so is an ideal site, not only for small groups of anglers but also for the organised club competitions. Dates could be fixed well in advance thus allowing clubs to produce fixture lists with others, and the large number of sturdy boats enabled all participants to get on the water and be ably rowed by two professional boatmen to each boat. It was an agreement that clubs would provide these worthies with sandwiches and beer but not with whisky, as otherwise they might not be in a fit state to get their 'gentlemen' back to the Kinross jetty at the end of the day, nor to row in the rough conditions which frequently prevail.

The oldest National Trout Fly-Fishing Competition in the world was held for the first time on Thursday, 1st July, 1880. The lead was given by the *West of Scotland Angling Club*, many of whose members were shareholders of the now defunct *Loch Leven Angling Association Limited* which, at that time, had the lease of the fishings on Loch Leven. Thirty-two anglers participated and landed 132 trout. This was the start of a competition which, with some exceptions in recent years, has been held annually except for the years of the First and Second World Wars. A further development was the International championship. This initially started with England in 1928 but four years later Wales and Ireland joined the tournament.

A delightful description of the *Edinburgh Angling Club* medal competition appears in the Winter, 1992 issue of *The Flyfishers' Journal*. Members of this club still religiously compete in this competition in the autumn, although salmon and sea trout are not as abundant as they were in former times.

The weigh-ins at the end of the day were very serious affairs and some clubs carried their own scales. *The Cockburn Angling Club* was presented with a chest with lock and key for holding their scales, etc. However, there is always a 'joker' and a Mr. Graham at one weigh-in at a *Cockburn Angling Club* competition produced an 8lb cod and three partans (crabs) but was disqualified as they were not yellow trout according to the rules!

Angling competitions were sometimes combined with other functions, and the *West of Scotland Angling Club* used to end its competition at Abington on the Clyde with races and other sports. On one occasion an outing coincided with Queen Victoria's birthday so, activated by feelings of intense loyalty, the club had a firework display at the end of the day.

On loch, river and stream anglers engage in fishing matches throughout the season from mid-March to the end of September then, when the trout are ready to spawn, they reel up their lines, take down their rods and start their indoor social engagements around the hotel and tavern dining table.

The cost of the dinners in the early 1880s varied between 4/- and 4/6d per head, although they were known to cost more and the fourth annual dinner of the *West of Scotland Angling Club* cost 11/10d and the Anniversary dinners were 13/-. Some clubs had their own stocks of wine and the *Ellem Fishing Club* held a good stock of claret at the White Swan Hotel in Duns but the last of this mysteriously disappeared during the years of the Second World War. Legend states that it was consumed by our 'Allies' stationed in the area! The *West of Scotland Angling Club* built up its nucleus of a wine cellar when, at the 1847 dinner, the President offered six bottles of champagne for members at the next outing on Loch Lomond. This stock was kept replenished by making wagers against each other and, as all bets were for the benefit of the Club, the loser was obliged to hand to the Club a bottle of champagne. Occasionally there would be group bets as when the bachelors challenged the married men and thirteen bottles were at stake. Sometimes there were freak bets as when, on 7th January, 1851, 'Mr. Harvey bets Mr.Bran a bottle of champagne that the mouth of the Garnock is south of the mouth of the Tweed.'

Some club dinners are renowned for their length and jollity and probably the *Hawick Angling Club* dinners hold the record for their length and insobriety. The proceedings start at 7.30 p.m. and continue well into the morning and are punctuated by song, recitations, accordion solos and stories. The Superintendent of the local constabulary is always invited so as to put a seal on the legality of a boisterous night.

The annual dinner is the event at which trophies and prizes for the various competitions and feats held during the fishing season are presented. Some of the prizes are elaborate and valuable while others have a more functional or ephemeral value. Those coming into the first category take the form of cups, medals and salvers. The *Ellem Fishing Club* medal has the names of all the winners since 1830 engraved on it and is now nine inches in diameter and is valued at well over £2,000. The winner is quick to confine it to the bank's safe for the year it is placed in his possession. The *Edinburgh Angling Club*, too, has a valuable medal. The *Phoenix Club* has, in addition to cups, silver salvers, coffee jugs and cigarette boxes, an interesting trophy called 'The Kettle'. It is a copper kettle reputed to have been left on Castle Island in Loch Leven by

Mary, Queen of Scots. It was anonymously presented to the club in 1967. The Kettle is presented by the club champion to the least fortunate club member of the season. When presenting the Kettle the club champion also gives a small tangible memento to the recipient and this has usually been a priest. Other interesting trophies include an oversized snooker cue known as the 'Charlie Brown', named after its donor and competed for annually by the *Trout Anglers' Club* members, and the Rhinocerous Poacher which consists of a whale's tooth mounted on a plinth and presented to the runner-up in the *Edinburgh Walton Angling Club* championship. *The Cockburn Angling Club* had, at one time, a wide range of trophies including wading stockings, oil painting, marble time-piece, bird cage and a wool mat. The wool mat appears to have been awarded annually to various parties until presumably it disintegrated.

Much of the charm of social occasions around the dining table is in the recounting of the season's exploits and remembering the pleasures of the waterside. Those with poetic leanings are more able to recapture these experiences and *The Edinburgh Angling Club* has immortalised many of its members' poems in a delightful book, which has run to three editions, entitled *The Songs of the Edinburgh Angling Club*. It first appeared in 1858 and a larger version in 1878. The third verse of the first poem – *The Call*- epitomises the spirit of the true angler:

> *I care not for honours, I care not for gain*
> *The path of ambition shall never tempt me;*
> *My days I would spend, free from sorrow and pain,*
> *Where Tweed pours its waters by sweet Fernielee,*
> *O, there would I wander, from morning till night*
> *With Rod and with Line the bright salmon to snare,*
> *Then repose on its banks till the last ray of light*
> *Leaves in shadow and stillness the old bridge of Yair.*

Angling clubs are not all 'fishing and frivolity' and many were established with a very sincere desire to protect and improve the fishing. For example, the *Gala Angling Association* was set up to prevent the illegal practice of netting and taking trout by other unfair means from the Gala and other tributaries of Tweed. The rules of the Association provided that (a) each member of the Club use every endeavour in his power to suppress all illegal destruction of freshwater trout in the River Gala and other tributaries of Tweed, and shall report such cases of illegal fishing to the committee; and (b) a reward of 10/- shall be given for every person taken in the act of illegal fishing, and a further reward of the same sum for every net taken in the act of fishing, payable upon conviction of offenders. *The West of Scotland Angling Club*, too, was concerned at the catching of fish in an illegal manner and out of season and also at the selling of 'foul and unseasonable' fish by fishmongers. They were particularly concerned at the illegal fishing on the Clyde and urged Clyde proprietors to form themselves into a *Clyde Protection Society*. The Club also instructed advertisements to be inserted in the Glasgow and local papers stating that if anyone infringed the Salmon Fisheries Acts the Club would see to it that they were 'brought to book.'

Many clubs to this day follow the good example set by their forebears in protecting their rivers from poaching and pollution, but both problems are still with us and the future of our fishing requires the vigilance of all club members.

Chapter 23 – **The Beginning**

The bombers were droning overhead. The youth, standing on the river bank, looked up from his fishing. He could see they were Lancasters and knew they were assembling prior to one of the thousand bomber raids. He watched them for a moment, his eyes watering with pride. He turned his gaze back to the river. No fish were rising even though it was a fine spring day. This was his first day out with his new fly rod and brand new Hardy's reel. What a difference from his previous gear. This had consisted of a 10½ft. coarse fishing rod with a wooden Nottingham reel. Prior to that it had been three garden canes from his friend's garden shed. Each cane of a slightly different diameter so that they fitted one in to the other. Then staples hammered in at intervals along the rod and an eye screw put in at the top of the smallest cane and bent slightly down. Two thick rubber bands secured the bakelite reel. A hunk of twisted line, a quill float and a gut cast completed the outfit. The quarry had been roach on bread paste and perch on red worm. The venue for outings being Plumpton Rocks near Harrogate, painted at one time by Turner.

The weather had been very bright for some days and the tackle shop told him to try bright flies and sold him some size 10 March Browns with a body of silver tinsel. It was a lovely stretch of the Nidd lying a mile or so upstream of Knaresborough. The river was pretty heavily tree-lined with good pools alternating with stretches of fast water. As no fish were rising he waded into the water just where a run of fast water was easing as it entered the pool. A sycamore tree whose buds were just opening sheltered him. His wet fly cast consisted of a Silver March Brown as tail fly, Orange Partridge on the second dropper and a Waterhen Bloa on the top dropper. He cast his line out as best he could owing to the overhanging branches of the sycamore and let the line come round until it was below him and held out in the current the length of the rod from the bank. He gradually let more line out and worked the cast by moving his rod upstream and then downstream. Suddenly his line was pulled tight, his rod bent and the reel screamed. He had a fish on! The tree didn't help and, as he couldn't follow the fish, he had to play it against the current. Everything was in favour of the fish but gradually, with a great deal of patience, the fish was brought struggling into slack water and, after one or two attempts, lifted into the rickety net given him by a friend. He clambered onto the bank with the fish wriggling. He picked up a flat stone and carefully hit the fish on the head. It was a beautiful golden trout of about ¾lb. with lovely markings. He carefully wrapped the fish up in some sandwich paper and waded in again. Using the same technique he caught two slightly smaller trout. The silver tinsel on the March Brown by that time had unwound from the body and was hanging on by a thread. He decided to call it a day – a memorable day. The sound of aircraft had gone and the country was peaceful. In the distance a blackbird was singing. He walked up to where he'd left his bike and set off for home.

His parents admired the trout nicely laid out on one of his mother's old plates and said they would have them tomorrow for dinner. His mother was a great one for reading what the stars foretold in the *Daily Mirror* and later that evening looked up from her paper. "Dearest, you know what it says under your stars – Pisces – 'You have recently taken up a pursuit that will influence your future career'."

"In which case," said his father rather sarcastically looking over the top of *The Times* and always keen to get a dig in about his son's scholastic achievements and future career, "The recording angels better be sharpening their pencils!"